TOOL*SMARTS*

Workshop
Dust Control

>> *Install a Safe, Clean System for Your Home Woodshop*

Table of Contents

Hazards of Wood Dust

ALLERGIES, FIRE HAZARD, MESS—YOU CAN AVOID IT ALL

There is no doubt that wood dust is messy and annoying, but now there also is research showing that decades of exposure to fine wood dust can contribute to nasal and lung cancer. These cases are among factory workers who breathed dust day in and day out for many years. For the weekend woodworker, however, allergies are a much more likely problem. Allergies can develop quickly, even among occasional woodworkers, and the symptoms worsen with increased exposure.

Besides the common sneezing attacks, allergic reactions can take the form of skin rashes, sinusitis, bronchitis, and asthma. The woods most likely to lead to reactions are red cedar, oak, redwood, mahogany, walnut and many tropical species. However, all wood dusts are potential allergens, and the fine dust—10 micron and smaller—is the worst offender. If you've ever talked to a hard-core woodworker who's been forced to abandon his shop forever because of allergies, it will make you a true believer in dust control.

Besides the health issues, we encourage dust control because dust is a fire hazard. Sparks can occur from faulty wiring or a grinder, dust can settle on hot light fixtures, plus there's always danger from oily rags. All of these have caused numerous shop fires. If your shop is in your home, you should be doubly careful.

One frequently neglected fire-safety practice is to empty your dust collector after each day's use. You don't want a spark to smolder in that pile of dry dust.

If you want to do woodworking for the long haul, get your dust—especially the fine dust—under control. The best approach (in order of priority):

- Wear an effective dust mask.
- Use a vacuum to collect dust from finish sanders, routers, and other portable power tools (page 10).
- Use a dust collector with generous felt bags on stationary machines (page 24).
- Invest in an air scrubber (page 88).

RESPIRATORS FOR WOODWORKERS

A paper dust mask can be an effective antidote to breathing wood dust, but only if the device makes a good seal with your face. Otherwise, you'll just breathe the dust leaking in around the edges of the mask. For woodworkers who wear beards, an effective seal is almost impossible.

However, there is an answer: a powered respirator that pumps filtered air into a mask. This creates positive pressure inside the mask and prevents any dust-laden outside air from leaking inside. The stream of filtered air flows down the inside of the visor and across the face, keeping you cool and preventing the visor from fogging. For a list of suppliers, please see page 132.

Vacuum the Dust

The first line of defense against woodshop dust and debris is the shop vacuum. Use it to pick up the dust and chips produced by your woodworking machines. You also can connect most shop vacs to portable power tools and small woodworking machines, to collect the debris as it's created.

« A large shop vac makes short work of this mess of chips. A smaller machine would be liable to choke, however.

by GEORGE VONDRISKA *and* TOM CASPAR

Shop Vacuums

HOW TO CHOOSE THE RIGHT VACUUM FOR YOUR SHOP

If you haven't test-driven a shop vacuum in a while, get ready to be impressed. These aren't Grandpa's machines. Their filtration is better, their motors are quieter and their power is outstanding.

Choosing the right vacuum for your shop is not easy, though. There are so many models! We'll cover some broad categories of vacuums so you'll get an idea of what your budget will buy. We'll also take a closer look at a few selected vacuums that you may find useful in your shop.

NOT JUST FOR CLEANUP

These days, workshop vacuums have two main uses: general cleanup and dust collection from small tools. The latest sanders, routers, plate joiners and router tables have dust ports for hooking up to a vacuum. Teamed with a dust collector for your tablesaw, planer and jointer, a good vacuum should capture most of the small, unhealthy dust particles these tools make before the dust becomes airborne.

Both uses impose different requirements on a vacuum. For cleanup (or for a router table), you need lots of air flow for gobbling up a large pile of

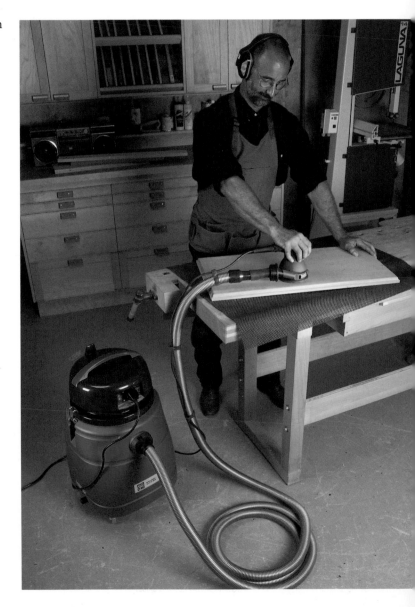

wood chips and lots of suction for picking up heavy chunks of wood and other debris, like nails and screws. A large, 2¼-in. hose is ideal. For dust collection from a portable power tool, you don't need as much air flow or suction, but you do need a smaller diameter, flexible hose and a switch that automatically turns on the vacuum when you turn on the tool. Most vacuums are better at one job than another, so when you look over the field, ask yourself whether you want a vacuum just for cleanup, just for tools or for both.

Which vacuum is the most powerful? This is a complicated question. Vacuuming power is a combination of two forces: suction and air flow. We conducted a real-world test on the vacuums profiled here by measuring their ability to pick up roofing nails and sawdust. The more nails a vacuum could pick up in a given amount of time, the better its suction power. The more sawdust it could pick up, the higher its air flow.

Pleated paper filters are standard on most vacuums. Pleating adds surface area, which increases the filter's effectiveness. You've got to keep the filter clean, though, or the vacuum will lose power.

» Hook up a shop vacuum to a portable power tool and you may never have to breathe dust again. Some vacuums have hoses and switches specifically designed for this setup, but even an ordinary vacuum can be outfitted with the right equipment to collect virtually all the dust from a sander, plate joiner or router.

FEATURES

Power

Amperage represents the amount of electrical current used by a vacuum's motor. It's a rough indication of a vacuum's ability to pick up dust and debris. Vacuums with 8-amp motors or greater are more than adequate for collecting dust from a sander; 11- to 12-amp vacuums perform much better at collecting dust from a router table or gulping big piles of sawdust from the floor.

Capacity

The bigger the tub, the less often you'll have the unpleasant chore of emptying it. A big tub also helps keep your filter clean. That's important, because a clogged filter leads to a loss in vacuuming power. Most filters hang inside the tub, right under the motor. If the tub is small, the filter can quickly become surrounded by and packed with dust and debris. If the tub is large, the filter stays out of the dust longer.

Filtration

The vacuum you choose should have, at minimum, a pleated HEPA-rated filter (photo, left). HEPA stands for High-Efficiency Particulate Air. A HEPA filter should remove 99.97 percent of the particles 0.3 microns and larger, but few if any filters are independently certified to meet this standard. Nevertheless, it's the best filter for your vacuum and lungs, because the smallest dust particles are the most hazardous to your health.

Types of Shop Vacuums

GENERAL-PURPOSE VACUUMS

These vacuums are fantastic for cleaning up the shop, but their large, stiff hoses are much too unwieldy for connecting to portable power tools. General-purpose vacuums typically come with a kit that includes a floor wand and other cleaning tools. Spend another $70 for a tool-actuated switch and a small hose, though, and you've got a machine that could both clean the floor and hook up to a tool.

General-purpose vacuums come in a wide range of sizes. Increased horsepower and capacity usually go hand in hand. We've somewhat arbitrarily divided them into three groups:

Small Vacuums
1 to 2 peak hp, 6 to 8 amps, 2 gallons, $30 to $70

These machines are short and lightweight. You can easily tuck one under a bench or carry it outside to clean the car. They're inexpensive, so you can afford to dedicate one to a specific tool that creates small amounts of dust, like a miter saw. These are the least effective general-purpose machines for cleaning a very messy shop, however. They don't have the high air flow of their larger cousins, and the small tub fills quickly. Unfortunately, most of them are louder than other vacuums in our test and easier to tip over.

Midsize Vacuums
3 to 5 peak hp, 8 to 10 amps, 7 to 9 gallons, $75 to $100

Midsize vacuums are just fine for collecting the small volume of dust a portable power tool makes. They've got plenty of power for this job. For general cleanup, they'll hold much more sawdust and debris than a small vacuum, so you don't have to empty as often. However, as with a small vacuum, the midsize machine's filter hangs inside a relatively small tub and can quickly become surrounded by debris. The filter usually clogs up faster than one would in a large machine.

Large Vacuums
6 to 6.5 peak hp, 10 to 12 amps, 10 to 18 gallons, $120 to $180

If you've got the space to store it, and you're only going to own one, look for a vacuum in this class. These vacuums have lots of power and capacity for tackling even the largest piles of wood shavings and cut-offs. No other vacuum is as versatile. Equipped with an additional small hose and a tool-actuated switch, these vacuums can easily handle portable power tools, a disc sander, and most operations on a router table.

TOOL-ACTUATED VACUUMS

These vacuums are generally more expensive than general-purpose machines, but they're a real pleasure to use. They have plenty of air flow for picking up dust from a portable power tool. When attached to your sander or router, the vacuum automatically starts up when you turn on the tool and shuts down a few seconds after you switch off the tool. Sweet! There's one limitation, though. The combined amperage of the vacuum and tool must be within the wall outlet's amperage limit.

Tool-actuated vacuums have more great features, too. They're much quieter than general-purpose vacuums. They typically come with a long, super-flexible, small-diameter hose, perfect for connecting to portable power tools. Some come with a static-discharge hose, which prevents you from getting a nasty static shock. Some models have built-in mechanisms for shaking dust off the filter, so you don't have to remove the filter as often for cleaning. All models have a two-stage motor with an air bypass that helps extend a motor's life. Most models accept paperbag prefilters.

If your woodworking habits leave you with big piles of debris in the shop, you'll find that tool-actuated vacuums aren't as effective at shop cleanup as the largest general-purpose vacuums are, unless you sweep first. The tool-actuated models have less suction power for picking up chunks of wood. In addition, their small hoses can plug with small pieces of wood (though some vacuums have optional large hoses). Tool-actuated vacuums usually don't come with floor-cleaning accessories, such as a sweep or brush. A typical accessory kit costs about $60.

9 to 12 amps,
9 to 15 gallons,
$300 to $400

General-Purpose or Tool-Actuated?

We like both types of machine, but for different reasons. Here's how they stack up:

■ **Price.** Large general-purpose vacuums cost about half as much as tool-actuated vacuums. The equation stays the same when you add helpful accessories to both types: $70 for a small hose and tool-switch for a general-purpose machine, $60 for a floor-cleaning kit for a tool-actuated machine.

■ **Versatility.** Large general-purpose vacuums do a bang-up job cleaning a messy floor that is full of wood chips and debris. But you must purchase an accessory kit for use with portable power tools. With a tool-actuated machine, you should sweep up big chips and cut-offs before vacuuming; however, the vacuum is always ready to go with a portable power tool.

■ **Noise.** Tool-actuated vacuums are noticeably quieter than large general-purpose machines.

■ **Filtration.** Large general-purpose vacuums have filters that can easily clog because they hang down in the tub. You must bang the filter to clean it. Some filters on tool-actuated vacuums sit above the tub and can be cleaned without opening the tub. And some models have a built-in filter shaker.

We like a vacuum that can accept a paper bag prefilter (photo, right). The paper bag fits inside the tub. Once full, the entire bag is discarded. With a paper bag prefilter, you won't be banging your filter and releasing giant clouds of dust every time you empty the vacuum.

Air Bypass

The greatest enemy to a motor's life is excessive heat. The air that passes through a vacuum's fan also cools the motor. If the hose gets clogged, air doesn't move and the motor heats up. Some vacuums have a bypass air inlet that allows air to flow over the motor no matter what. If a vacuum has a two-stage motor (meaning it has two in-line fans) it usually has this bypass, also.

A paper bag prefilter inside your shop vacuum keeps your regular filter from filling up in a hurry. It also makes emptying the tub a lot easier. Bags are an option on many vacuums. Some have caps to cover the opening after you remove the bag.

EDITOR: TOM CASPAR • ART DIRECTION AND PHOTOGRAPHY: VERN JOHNSON, UNLESS NOTED • ILLUSTRATION: RYAN NELSON

Emptying a vacuum is a lot easier when its tub has a smooth rim. Some vacuums are more difficult to empty because their rims are stepped inward, like a pickle jar. To empty a stepped-rim vacuum, you must turn the tub completely over and shake it.

Easy-To-Empty Tub

It's easy to dump debris out of a tub that has a smooth wall (photo, left). It's harder with a tub that has a lip at the top, because you must tilt the tub much higher.

Swiveling Casters

Admit it. You know you're going to use the hose like a leash to tug the vacuum around your shop's obstacle course. We prefer four or five casters that can roll in any direction rather than two fixed wheels and two swiveling casters.

Blast Gate Manifold for Vac Hoses

In my small shop, I use a shop vacuum to collect dust from several tools. To cut down on the need to swap hoses, I built this manifold with two blast gates. Now I transfer suction with a flip of my wrist.

To make the box, I drilled holes for the hoses and rabbeted the box sides for the 1/8-in. blast gates. After cutting the end pieces to match the rabbets, I glued the box together on a long backplate for wall-mounting. I made blast gates from scraps of plastic, but hardboard would work just as well. To make the wooden handles, I sawed a kerf in an oversize blank, cut the handles from the blank and drilled holes for the screws.

—*Armand Niccolai*

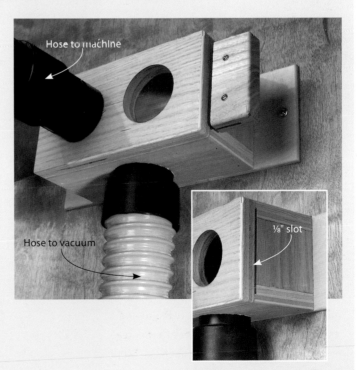

Hose to machine

Hose to vacuum

1/8" slot

EDITOR: TIM JOHNSON • ART DIRECTION: VERN JOHNSON • PHOTOGRAPHY: PATRICK HUNTER

by GEORGE VONDRISKA

Shop Vacuums for Portable Power Tools

LOOK MA, NO DUST CLOUDS

The biggest frustration I've encountered in trying to control the dust in my shop is this: You spend hundreds of dollars on a dust collector, hoses, blast gates, and whatnot, you hook it all up to your big machines and you're still only halfway there. You still need to deal with routers, plate jointers, belt sanders and finish sanders.

In the past few years, manufacturers have introduced specialized shop vacuums that allow you to collect dust right off these tools. If you hate dust, these vacuums will make you think you've died and gone to heaven. With one of these vacuums you can use a random-orbit sander for hours at 220 grit with no hint of a dust cloud.

The drawback is cost. These machines are twice as expensive as regular shop vacuums. You'll have to decide whether their specialized features are worth the extra cost, or whether you would be as well off with a general-purpose shop vacuum outfitted with aftermarket accessories that allow them to collect from power tools.

FEATURES YOU NEED IN A PORTABLE POWER-TOOL VACUUM

The specialized features needed to collect dust from sanders, routers, plate jointers, and the like are:

■ **Fine Filtration.** The tools you're hooking up to the vacuum produce very fine dust, and you don't want it just flying out the exhaust port. (I see a few bemused smiles out there—this really does happen!) The specialized power-tool vacuums filter down to 1-micron (according to the manufacturers). For regular shop vacuums, you can purchase an aftermarket Gore-Tex filter ($20) that also does the trick for fine particles.

■ **A Long, Flexible Hose.** You don't want the hose to make the tool awkward to handle, or tippy (bad news with a belt sander!) The smaller 1¼-in. or 1½-in. hoses are best for maneuverability. Because you often walk around with the tool, the longer the hose the better. For regular shop vacuums, long, flexible hoses are available as an aftermarket attachment ($30).

■ **Quiet.** It's bad enough to listen to a loud shop vacuum for a short spell of floor cleaning. Add that roar to the noise of a sander and you've got a recipe for insanity. Even the best hearing protectors aren't really enough. The specialized power-tool vacuums are fairly quiet, but for regular shop vacuums, you have to purchase an aftermarket muffler ($35).

■ **Tool-Actuated Switch.** With this feature, you plug your sander or other portable power tool into the vacuum, not into an outlet. When you turn on the tool, the vacuum turns on automatically. Usually the vacuum runs a bit after the dust-maker is shut off, just to clear the tool and the hose. Though certainly not essential, the tool-actuated switch is a handy feature for tools you start and stop a lot, like plate jointers and finish sanders.

《 This specialty vacuum can collect the dust directly from portable power tools such as routers, sanders, and plate joiners.

ART DIRECTION: PATRICK HELF • PHOTOGRAPHY: MIKE HABERMANN

WHAT'S THE DEAL WITH TOOL-ACTUATED SWITCHES?

Tool-actuated switches are convenient but they do have limitations. The receptacles on these machines have amperage limitations ranging from 6 amps to 19 amps. How does this limit what tools can plug into the vacuum? Here are some approximate tool amperages:

Finish sander	2 amps
Random orbit sander	2 amps
Belt sander	7 amps
Plate joiner	7 amps
1.5 hp router	11 amps
Miter saw	13 amps

Remember that the combined amperage of the tool and the vacuum can't exceed your circuit breaker's capacity. You may need to plug into separate outlets just to keep the amperage per circuit low.

Another option: If you choose a shop vacuum that doesn't have a tool-actuated switch, the Craftsman Automatic Power Switch lets you plug in a power tool and two accessories, like a light and vacuum. When the tool goes on, the accessories go on. The accessories continue to run three seconds after the tool is shut off. The switch can handle up to 15 amps. Get it at Sears for about $20.

by GEORGE VONDRISKA

Soup Up Your Shop Vacuum

HOOK UP TO ANY PORTABLE POWER TOOL WITH THIS SET OF ACCESSORIES

Most shop vacuums are big and powerful, like SUVs. These vacuums have tons of suction power for cleaning the mess on your floor, but their standard hoses and fittings are way too big to use with portable power tools. There's no way you're going to attach a stiff, heavy, 2¼-in. hose to a random-orbit sander! You need accessories that are small, lightweight and nimble, like a sports car. With this set of options, you can hook up nearly any workshop vacuum to any portable power tool. What a difference! No more choking sawdust—it's definitely the way to go.

VERSATILE HOSE

Super-flexible, long, lightweight and small in dia-meter—that's what you're looking for in a hose. This 1¼-in. hose from Shop Vac weighs less than 2 lbs., runs 18 ft. long and bends easily. The end that fits into your vacuum's tub is a standard 2¼-in. straight sleeve.

FINER FILTER

The smallest dust particles are the largest health hazard. To best capture sanding dust, switch from a standard filter to a high-efficiency particulate air (HEPA) filter. This CleanStream HEPA-grade fabric filter doesn't clog as easily as a paper HEPA filter and can be cleaned with water. These filters are machine-specific, so you'll need to buy one that fits your vacuum's make and model.

TOOL-ACTUATED SWITCH

This convenient gadget will really turn you on. Actually, it's your vacuum that automatically turns on whenever you fire up a power tool. Plug the Craftsman Automatic Power Switch into an outlet; then plug the tool and vacuum into the switch. It works just like the tool-actuated switch on a high-end vacuum. The vacuum starts up with the tool and runs an additional 2 to 3 seconds to clear the hose after you've turned off the tool. The switch is rated to handle a total of 15 amps for the vacuum plus a tool.

HOSE CLIPS

These handy clips from Fein bind together your tool's power cord and a 1¼-in. vacuum hose. Five clips are usually enough for an 18-ft. hose.

HOSE ADAPTERS

Chances are every power tool in your shop has a different size of dust port, right? It's time to buy a set of hose adapters. These two from Fein should be good for most situations.

- Cut the step adapter to custom-fit the inside or outside diameter of a dust port. The large end fits on the hose; the small end has a ⅞-in. inside diameter and 1¹⁄₁₆-in. outside diameter at the taper's end.
- The flexible rubber sleeve connects to a dust port that has approximately the same outside diameter as the end of the hose—about 1¼ in.

Flexible sleeve

Step adapter

Dedicated Dust Collection

Many woodworkers don't have central dust collection. Instead, they repeatedly have to haul their shop vacuum between tools. This is a big hassle with a chop saw, because you usually only need it for a couple of cuts at a time. The solution? Buy an inexpensive extra vacuum and put it under the chop-saw bench permanently. Buy a tool-actuated switch so the vacuum comes on automatically when you start the chop saw. It's not the most elaborate system, but it works!

—*Tom Caspar*

Tool-actuated switch

Dedicated vacuum

by JACK BESTE

Muffle Your Shop Vac

CARPET-LINED BOX EATS THE NOISE

This solution was sent to us by Jack Beste, President of WoodWrite, a company that makes automated pen lathes. His customers spend hours turning exotic woods, using a shop vacuum for dust control. The noise was terrible.

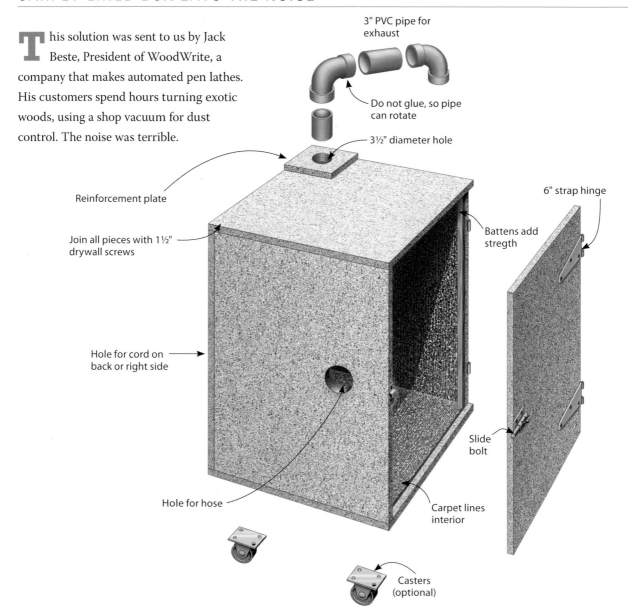

3" PVC pipe for exhaust

Do not glue, so pipe can rotate

3½" diameter hole

Reinforcement plate

6" strap hinge

Battens add stregth

Join all pieces with 1½" drywall screws

Hole for cord on back or right side

Slide bolt

Hole for hose

Carpet lines interior

Casters (optional)

The solution they've come up with is what we call a muffler box. It's dirt simple, dirt cheap ($40), but man, does it work! It's just a box, made from plywood or MDF, lined with old carpet and fitted with an exhaust hole on top. The casters and the pipe to direct the exhaust are optional.

The noise reduction from this muffler box is amazing. It's easy to have a normal conversation with the vacuum running right next to you, and to have the vacuum running for long periods of time without driving you batty. We don't know what this box does to the longevity of your vacuum's motor, but we have reports of people having their vacuum going all day long for days without ill effect.

You could build this box with the exhaust on the side so it doubles as a rolling worktable, or trick it out with holders for hose and tools. With a small $40 shop vacuum inside, you'd have yourself an inexpensive dedicated vacuum for your sanders and other portable power tools. Possibilities galore. This thing works.

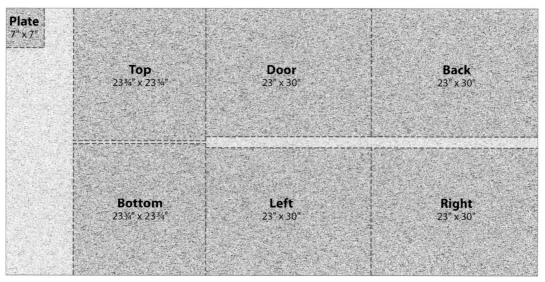

Plate
7" x 7"

Top
23¾" x 23¾"

Door
23" x 30"

Back
23" x 30"

Bottom
23¾" x 23¾"

Left
23" x 30"

Right
23" x 30"

Dimensions are for a 5-HP, 16-gallon Sears shop Vacuum. Alter to fit your machine.

MATERIALS LIST
- 1 sheet ¾" x ¾" MDF or plywood
- 4 battens of solid wood, ¾" x ¾" x 29"
- 4 battens of solid wood, ¾" x ¾" x 20¼"
- old carpet to line interior

HARDWARE
- 1 pr. 6" strap hinges
- 1 slide bolt
- 4 casters (optional)
- 8" PVC pipe, 3½" O.D.
- 2 PVC elbows
- 1½" drywall screws

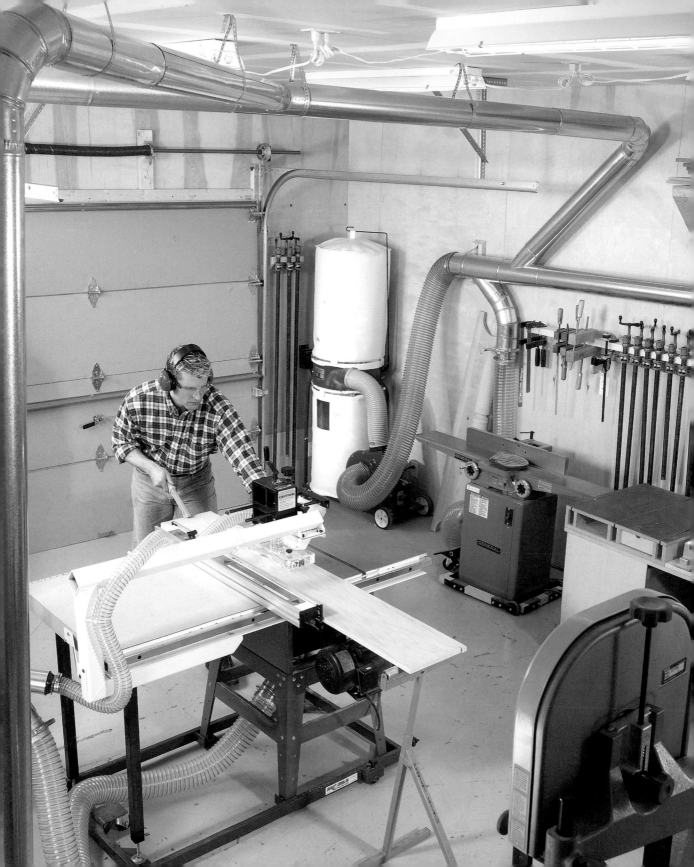

Collect the Dust

I n a busy shop, and in any shop with a lot of stationary woodworking machines, the shop-vac solution to dust control soon becomes too limited and too cumbersome. The logical step up is to a centralized dust-collection system. Ductwork and flexible hose connect each machine to a larger debris-collecting and air-filtering unit. A system of blast gates shifts the air flow to the machine you're currently using, closing off the air flow from elsewhere in the workshop. Systems like this used to be too expensive for the small workshop, but in the past 15 years a number of affordable central dust collection units have become available. In this section we'll show you how to specify and install one of these systems.

《 Every machine in this garage workshop connects to the central dust collector in the center of the photo. Chips and debris fall into the base unit, while the top-mounted filter bag cleans the air and returns it to the shop.

By DAVE MUNKITTRICK

Central Dust Collection

FIVE SIMPLE RULES FOR A DUST FREE SHOP

Small, one-person shops don't need complicated dust-collection systems. We'll show you how to get powerful collection at the lowest possible price without ever having to use a calculator. Even if your shop is shoehorned into a corner of your basement or garage, you can still enjoy the benefits of central dust collection. We turned to the experts at Oneida Air Systems (see Sources, page 132) for both the design and materials for our fully featured, small-shop dust-collection system. Our shop fits in one stall of a two-car garage, where the machines have to be moved against the walls to accommodate a car (photo at right).

ART DIRECTION: PATRICK HUNTER • PHOTOGRAPHY: BILL ZUEHLKE

Room for the Car

COST

The total cost for our system (excluding the dust collector) was under $1,000. Expect to spend about a day putting in the system. I know what you're thinking, "Wow, I can't afford that!" But, don't forget, we built a deluxe system with floor sweeps and ductwork running to each machine. You could cut the cost of our system in half simply by doing what I do in my shop at home: sharing. It takes about five seconds to pull the flex hose off one machine and hook it up to another. For example, the 4-in. flex hose to the tablesaw could easily be shared with the bandsaw and the lathe. That would eliminate the run to the bandsaw, plus a bunch of expensive flex-hose, blast gates and fittings. In addition, we could have stopped the wall run at the chop saw instead of going all the way to the workbench.

SMALL SHOP SYSTEMS ARE SIMPLER THAN YOU THINK

Designing a central dust-collection system for a small shop is really straightforward. Complex calculations involving cubic feet per minute, air velocity and static pressure are important for large industrial systems with long runs to big machines all running at the same time. A small, one-person shop is much simpler. The runs are short (our longest run was about 25 ft.) and only one machine runs at a time. The amount of air needed for good dust collection is relatively small. A system needs to pull about 500 cubic feet per minute (cfm) at the farthest machine to offer effective dust collection. A typical 1½- or 2-hp dust collector with a 5- or 6-in. inlet and a 12-in. impeller is capable of delivering enough air in a small system to collect from tools like a 10-in. tablesaw, a 15-in. planer, a 16-in. bandsaw, or an 8-in. jointer.

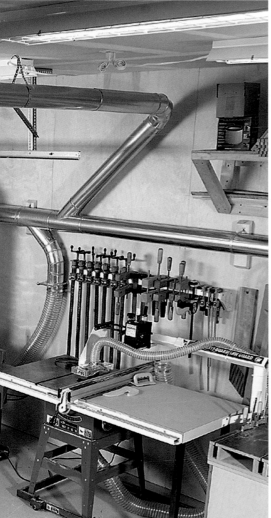

You can have a central dust-collection system! Just because your shop is small it doesn't mean a central system isn't practical. We built our system in a single stall of a double garage. The ductwork goes along the wall and ceiling and all the tools are on mobile bases.

FIVE DESIGN RULES

A well-designed central dust-collection system is built like a freeway. The road has to be wide enough to handle a large volume of traffic (5-in. ductwork to all machines). Turns need to be gentle so traffic can move at a high speed without crashing (large-radius elbows). Intersections should use entrance ramps that allow traffic to gently merge (45-degree wyes for drops and branches).

Too often people build their dust-collection systems like back-country roads with narrow lanes and abrupt, 90-degree turns. They accept inferior results because they've never known what their dust collector is capable of delivering with a well-designed system.

Rule #1
USE 5" PIPE

Using undersized ducts and fittings is the number one mistake people make. For a dust collector, it's like trying to drink a malt with a cocktail straw. Undersized ductwork restricts the cfm performance of your dust collector. Stick with 5-in. ductwork for small systems. Running 5-in. ductwork to all the machines maximizes the cfm performance of even a small central system.

=

Undersized
Ductwork

Properly Sized
Ductwork

Rule #2
KEEP IT STRAIGHT

Minimize the number of bends. Each 90-degree turn creates as much resistance to airflow as 9 ft. of 5-in. straight pipe.

Rule #3
USE FITTINGS DESIGNED FOR DUST COLLECTION

Dust-collection fittings are designed to efficiently carry dust-laden air at about 40 mph. Just like a car, air moving at high speed can't take sharp turns without running into trouble. The large-radius elbow is more than three times as efficient as the sharp turn found on the HVAC elbow. Which turn would you rather make at 40 mph? HVAC fittings are designed to carry air at a slow speed. Their sharp turns and 90-degree intersections create a ton of drag in a dust-collection system.

Heating and air conditioning

Dust collection

4" Flange

Rule #4
CHANGE THE DUST FITTINGS ON YOUR TOOLS

Manufacturers sometimes put a dust port where it fits best, not where it works best. More often than not, the ports are undersized as well. A few simple alterations can make a huge difference in how much dust gets left behind on hard-to-collect-from tools such as bandsaws. Use 4-in. ports wherever possible; 5 in. is even better.

Rule #5
YOU DON'T NEED A BIG DUST COLLECTOR

People agonize over this selection but it's really not that tough. For your basic shop under 1,000 sq. ft., where only one machine will be on at a time, a 1½- to 2-hp collector with a 5-in. or 6-in. inlet and a 12-in. fanwheel will do the job. In our tests, the *American Woodworker* editors liked the Oneida 1½- or 2-hp cyclone collector.

Installation

A central dust-collection system is built like a freeway with wide lanes, entrance ramps and gentle turns.

Even if you've never dealt with ductwork before, you won't have any trouble putting up your system. Be sure to wear leather gloves when handling sheet-metal parts. The metal edges can be razor sharp.

Specialty Tools and Hardware

There are a couple of specialized tools you'll want for this job (photo below).

The only power tools you'll need are a drill for fastening the sections and a jigsaw for cutting the pipe to length. If you don't own a jigsaw, a reciprocating saw or a pair of tin snips will do the trick.

Start at the Collector

Most 1½- to 2-hp collectors have 5-in. inlets. It's best to run 5-in.-dia. pipe all the way to the tool, and use a reducer to step down to a 4-in. port, if necessary.

If your collector has a 6-in. inlet, start with a 6-in. line. After the first branch, step down to 5 in. and stick with that diameter until you get to the machines. A common mistake is to run 6 in. everywhere. Just because a 1½- or 2-hp collector has a 6-in. inlet, doesn't mean it has the power to run a central system made entirely with 6-in. pipe. Also, most small shop tools have 4-in. ports. When the airflow from a 4-in. port hits the 6-in. duct, the air speed is almost cut in half. The slow air speed can result in dust settling out in your duct.

Hand crimper

#8 x ½" Self-tapping hex-head sheet metal screws

Nut-Driver

Metal hanger strap

A few specialized tools and hardware are needed for installing metal ductwork. A hand crimper is a must-have. It'll set you back about $30, but when you need one, nothing else will do.

#8 x ½-in. self-tapping hex-head sheet metal screws and a nut-driver make attaching the pipe sections a breeze.

Metal hanger strap is the least-expensive way to hang duct from your walls or ceiling.

Anatomy of a Central Dust-Collection System for a Small Shop

While each system will be unique, all small-shop systems have certain elements in common.

Ours starts out with 6-in. duct running from the dust-collector inlet. At the second branch, the line steps down to 5 in. for the rest of the system. 45-degree wyes are used for the line branches to each tool. Large-radius elbows create direction changes. Blast gates turn the suction on and off at each machine. Flex hose allows mobile machines to be moved without having to disconnect from the system. Reducers are used to step down the 5-in. duct to fit 4-in.

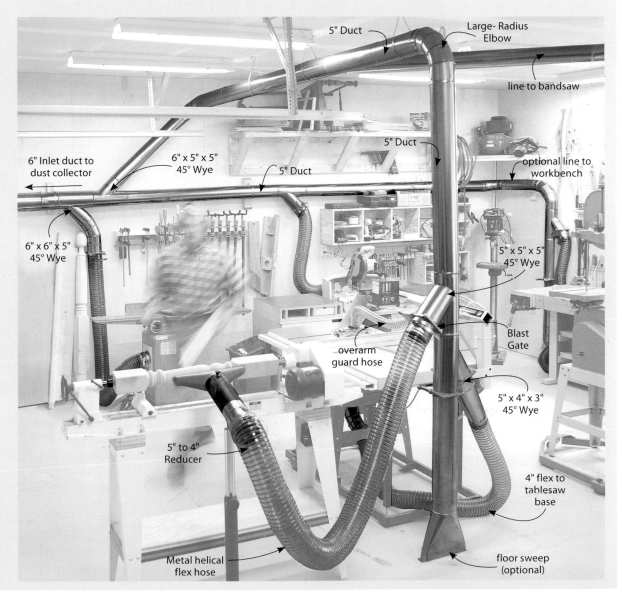

5" Duct

Large-Radius Elbow

line to bandsaw

6" Inlet duct to dust collector

6" x 5" x 5" 45° Wye

5" Duct

5" Duct

optional line to workbench

6" x 6" x 5" 45° Wye

5" x 5" x 5" 45° Wye

overarm guard hose

Blast Gate

5" x 4" x 3" 45° Wye

5" to 4" Reducer

4" flex to tablesaw base

Metal helical flex hose

floor sweep (optional)

If your shop is larger than 500 sq. ft. or you have a large machine like an 18-in. planer or a 24-in. drum sander, play it safe and buy a 2-hp collector with a 6-in. or larger inlet. Big tools like an 18-in. planer or a 24-in. drum sander will max out a small system. Locate big-draw tools as close to the dust collector as possible and run 6-in. duct right to the tool.

Assemble and Hang the Ductwork

The straight pipe we used has to be assembled, but it's no big deal. It takes a matter of seconds to snap together a section of pipe (right). Run the pipe with the crimped end pointing downstream toward the collector. We recommend mounting blocks and metal hanger strap to secure the duct to the wall (below).

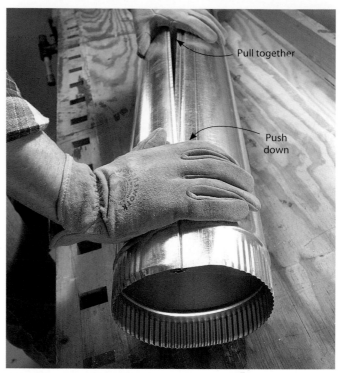

Pull together

Push down

A little downward pressure is the key to snapping together straight pipe. Start at the crimped end and slip the male edge into the female edge. Apply downward pressure on the seam as you move along the length of the pipe. Don't worry if the seam doesn't lock at first, somewhere beyond the halfway point the whole pipe will "snap" together.

2 x 4 Mounting Block

Hanger Strap

Install the pipe on the wall with a metal hanger strap attached to a 2x4 mounting block. Space the blocks every 4 to 5 ft. The blocks keep the pipe out from the wall a bit so it's a lot easier to fit and hang each section. Secure the pipe to the blocks by driving a #8 x 1½-in. screw through a loop of metal hanger strap.

Those Blasted Gates

Periodically, fine dust and sawdust accumulates in my plastic dust collector blast gates, preventing the gates from fully closing. Because the gates are permanently molded into the housing, I can't take them apart to clean them. Removing a small triangle at each of the bottom corners of the housing allows the vacuum in the dust collector hose to flush out this debris. Even though there are now "holes" in the blast gates, I haven't noticed any appreciable loss in performance, though you could cover the openings with duct tape and periodically remove the tape to clear the sawdust.

—*Carl Freeland*

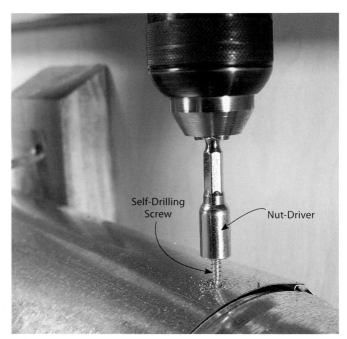

Secure joints with #8 x ½ in. self-tapping hex-head screws. A nut-driver and a cordless drill make quick work of fastening pipe sections without predrilling.

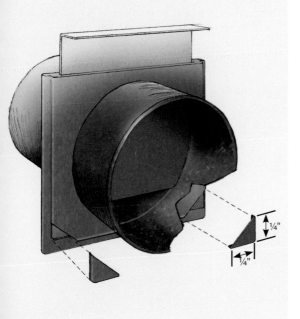

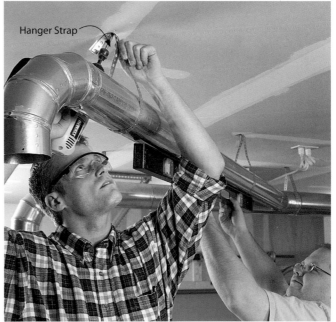

Suspend pipe from the ceiling with metal hanger strap. Cut the strap extra long, and have a helper hold the pipe level. Adjust the length of your loop and secure with a long screw into the rafters.

To join the pipe and fittings we found self-drilling sheet metal screws to be just the ticket. Don't worry about the screw ends protruding into the pipe, they're too small to matter. Use metal hanger strap every 3 to 4 ft. to suspend the ductwork from the ceiling, as shown on the previous page.

45-Degree Wyes

Use 45-degree wyes to create drops to each machine and to start branch lines (page 31). These are the "entrance ramps" to your dust-collection freeway. They allow the air stream to change directions without abrupt turns.

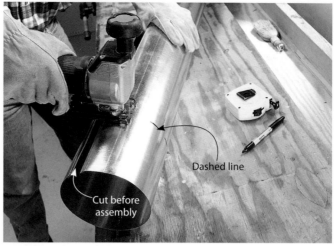

Dashed line

Cut before assembly

Cut pipe to length with a jigsaw and a metal-cutting blade. If you're using snap-lock pipe, do the cutting before the pipe is put together. Use a felt-tip pen to mark the pipe with a series of dashes. Cutting the pipe makes a racket, so be sure to wear hearing protection.

Plastic or Metal?

We strongly recommend metal ductwork. It's clearly superior to PVC or plastic because:

1. Only metal pipe comes in 5-in. dia., the ideal size for small-shop systems.

2. Metal systems are much easier to disassemble and change as your shop evolves.

3. Static electric build-up in PVC and plastic ductwork can be a problem. We've all experienced the jolt a shop-vacuum hose can give. Imagine what a dust-collection system can do. Plus, all commercial codes require metal pipe for wood-dust collection.

4. The metal ductwork we used is only about 20-percent more expensive than PVC in sizes over 4 in.

This 26-gauge metal ductwork is designed specifically for dust collection.

PVC plastic is designed to carry water.

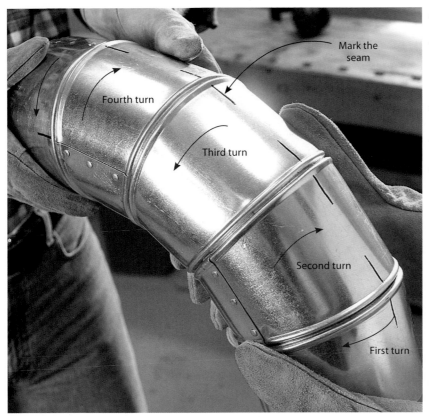

Fourth turn

Third turn

Mark the seam

Second turn

First turn

A few quick twists will turn a 90-degree elbow into a 45-degree elbow. Mark each seam along the spine of the elbow. Turn the first section about 90 degrees while a helper holds the other sections still. Then, turn the first and second sections together, 90 degrees in the opposite direction. Continue until each section has been turned.

Cutting the Pipe

Cutting pipe with a jigsaw makes one heck of a racket. Don't be surprised if the noise attracts curious neighbors and family members. (It's the perfect opportunity to ask for a little help putting up that ceiling run.) We found a jigsaw with a metal-cutting blade gave the best results with the least hassle.

Elbows

Use adjustable, large-radius elbows to make those gentle turns. They cost less than fixed elbows ($10 vs. $17) and because they're adjustable, there's no need to special order 45- or 30-degree elbows. The first time I tried to change a 90-degree into a 45-degree elbow, I ended up with a mess. The key is to turn each section 90 degrees and alternate the direction each section is turned to produce a smooth 45-degree elbow (above). To get a 30-degree sweep, turn each section 120 degrees instead of 90 degrees.

Tip: Loosen the joints by gently tapping the ends of the elbow on a flat surface.

Predrilled flange

Blast Gate

Thumb Screw

Blast-Gate Adapter

Flex Hose

Blast gates act like an on/off switch to control the airflow to each machine. Install your blast gate so the thumbscrew tightens the plate toward the dust collector. Blast-gate adapters add length to the stubby flange on the blast gate for easier attachment of the flex hose. Note: you must predrill through the cast-aluminum blast gate.

Blast Gates and Flex Hose

At the point where a line branches off to serve a single machine (usually at a 45-degree wye) we added a blast gate, blast-gate adapter and flex hose (above). Attach the flex hose with adjustable hose clamps. Flex hose is expensive ($5 per ft. for 5-in. dia.) so keep it as short as possible. If you know your machine isn't going anywhere, run rigid pipe right to the tool.

We recommend using flex hose with an imbedded metal coil and keeping the lengths under 5 ft. The metal coil and short length will keep electrostatic discharge to a minimum. To completely ground the system, just peel back the plastic to expose the wire at each end. Bend the exposed wire into a loop and screw it to the metal pipe on one end and the machine's dust port on the other.

Seal all the joints with silicone. If your pipe seems a bit oily, clean the joints with a little vinegar first.

Turn Your Dust Collector on Its Head!

I use my 2-hp dust collector as a central unit. Turning the collector upside down and hanging it from the ceiling allows me to hook up my trunk line without any elbows. It also saves on floor space and because the barrel handles the chips, there's no loss of CFM from a full bag. But best of all, this system eliminates the dust storm created when removing a full bag.

Replace the metal base with ¾-in. plywood sized to span your floor joists. (The old base makes a great shop cart!) With the help of a couple friends, bolt the whole assembly to your floor joists. To help dampen vibration, drill out the centers of six 1½-in.-thick rubber stoppers to use as washers between the base and the bottom of your joists. Finally, remove the fabric bottom of one bag and use a cinch strap to attach it to a barrel with an approximately 20-in.-diameter top.

Rubber stoppers are available at most hardware stores for about $4 apiece. You can pick up used barrels for $6 to $10. Look under "barrels" in the Yellow Pages.

—*Ross Peterson*

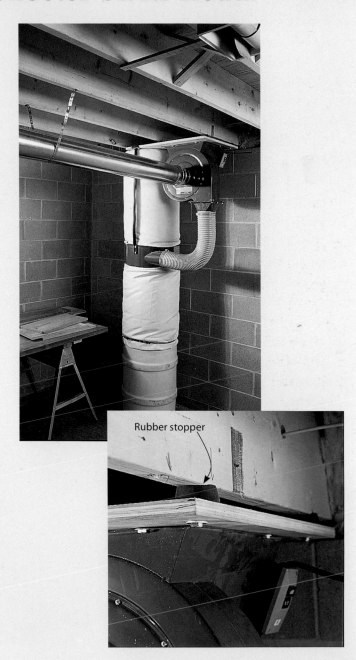

Rubber stopper

Modifying the Dust Ports on Your Machines

You'll find most of the dust ports on your machines require some modification. For example, in our shop, we swapped out the 4-in. plastic port on our jointer with a 5-in. flange bolted to a piece of plywood. We also added a 4-in. dust port to the bandsaw and made a hood for the chop saw (next page).

We split the 5-in. duct to the tablesaw with a 5 in. x 4 in. x 3 in. 45-degree wye joint and a 3- to 2-in. reducer. A 4-in. hose collects from the open area at the base of the saw while a 2-in. hose collects off of the overarm guard (photo page 31). The overarm guard makes a huge difference. It literally captures and whisks away all that stuff that gets thrown back at you from the saw blade.

Machines with a 4-in. dust port require a reducer fitting. Place a reducer as close to the machine as possible to ensure maximum cfm to the machine.

Once everything's attached, you'll be free at last from the tyranny of the broom and dust mask! No more dust tracked all over the house either. One last tip—get a remote control for the dust collector. With your new dust-collection system and a remote, woodworking's never been so good.

Hand Crimper

Use a hand crimper for the occasional situation where the pipe needs a crimped end, for example, to make your own blast-gate adapters.

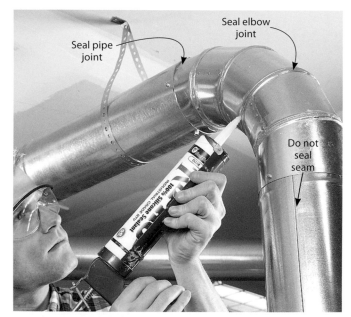

Seal pipe joint

Seal elbow joint

Do not seal seam

Seal all the joints with silicone caulk. Adjustable elbows, blast gates and pipe joints all leak air. That many joints leaking a little air adds up to a big cfm loss in your line. Note: It is not necessary to seal the snap-lock seams along the length of the duct.

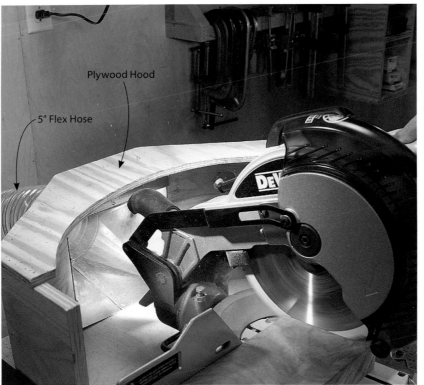

Some tools require custom-made dust ports. For our miter saw, for example, we built a simple plywood hood, with a large 5-in. port at the back. The powerful airflow from a well-designed central system makes this possible. Almost nothing escapes this dust trap.

Plywood Hood

5" Flex Hose

Dust Bag Hangers

When it came time to rehang the bag on my dust collector, I always wished I had five hands. One day I had an idea: I made five hooks out of a wire coat hanger. I simply pull the bag over the dust collector's flange, slip the hangers through the bag's belt loops and then adjust and tighten the bag belt.

—*John King, Jr.*

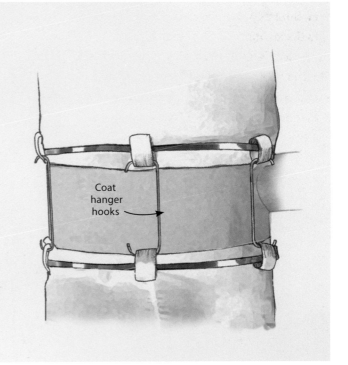

Coat hanger hooks

Clever Duct Tricks

THE RIGHT PIPE

Your worst nightmare: Sparks in a dust collector send your shop sky high! Not to worry. Choose metal pipe instead of PVC and you won't have to fret about sparks from static electricity. You shouldn't be surprised to hear that the Uniform Mechanical Code (a building code followed by most jurisdictions in the U.S.) forbids using PVC pipe for dust collection.

Look for 24- or 26-gauge metal heating pipe at any home center. Twenty-four-gauge pipe is thicker and should be used on powerful central systems whose suction might cause thinner 26-gauge pipes to collapse. You can easily cut this stuff with tin snips and it's cheap. You'll pay around 75 cents per foot for 4-in. dia. straight pipe in both thicknesses.

SEAL THE JOINTS

Metal pipe seams to leak air like crazy. After you've screwed your pipes together, seal the joints with silicone caulk. But first, clean the pipe with vinegar, or the silicone won't stick.

BIGGER BENDS MOVE MORE AIR

Join two standard 90-degree elbows together to make one super elbow! Why? For maximum efficiency. The turning radius of a dust collection pipe should be 1½ to 2 times the diameter of the pipe itself. A standard 90-degree elbow by itself takes too sharp a turn. Elbows can be twisted to form any angle, so bend two into 45-degree turns and join them together.

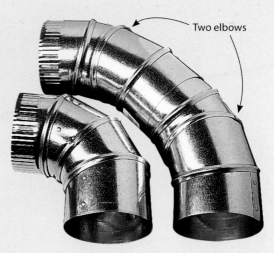

Two elbows

"Y" SHAPED FITTINGS ARE BEST

Don't you hate getting held up in your car at a crowded intersection? Dust has the same problem trying to enter the main run of a central dust collection system. Give it a freeway on-ramp by installing a Y fitting rather than a T fitting. T fittings create more turbulence in the air passing through them, so you get less suction. A 45-degree Y is more efficient, and a 30-degree Y is best.

Position the Y so it comes off the side or top of the main branch. If the Y points down, material passing through the main run will fall into the branch run when the branch's blast gate is closed.

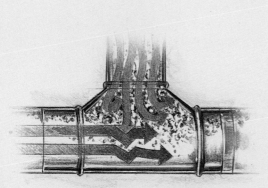
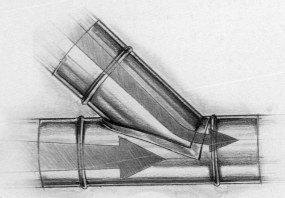

by ED KRAUSE AND DAVE MUNKITTRICK

Dust Collectors for a Small Shop

ONLY A FEW COLLECT THE MOST-HAZARDOUS DUST

Wood dust is a health hazard, and the worst dust is the stuff you can't see. Dust collectors seem like an easy answer to the problem. But do they do the job? Most of the collectors we tested collected chips just fine, but instead of collecting the fine dust, most of them actually emitted it! We'll tell you which collectors made the grade at collecting dust, and why. We'll also show what can be done to transform a dust spewer into an effective dust collector.

There are a lot of dust collectors out there. We limited this test to machines most likely to be used in a small shop—1- to 2-hp models costing less than $1,000.

We examined two crucial aspects of dust collection: 1. How well the machines pull in dust and chips at the source (air volume as measured in cubic feet per minute or cfm) and 2. How well the collectors contain the dust they collect.

IN A SINGLE-STAGE COLLECTOR

the chips and dust travel through the impeller and accumulate in the bags, which double as a filter medium. One big drawback to single-stage collectors is the drop in cfm performance that occurs as the lower bag fills with chips and dust.

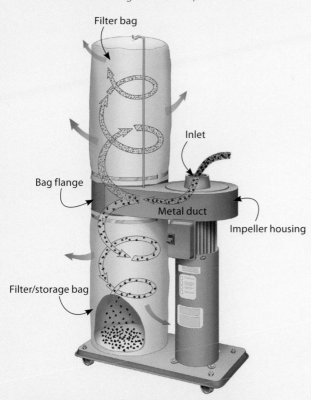

Filter bag

Inlet

Bag flange

Metal duct

Impeller housing

Filter/storage bag

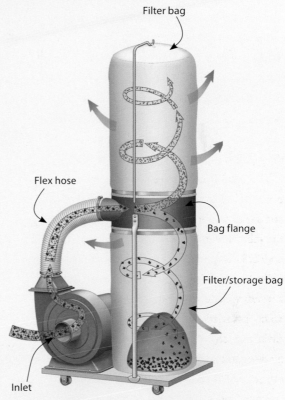

Filter bag

Flex hose

Bag flange

Filter/storage bag

Inlet

1-HP, Single-stage collectors have smaller bags that require more frequent emptying. But their small size is an asset in a shop where floor space is at a premium. The impeller housing is connected directly to the bag flange via a short metal duct. We found this design to be far less prone to dust leaks than the larger 1½-hp and 2-hp models with a flex-hose attachment. The 1-hp collectors perform best when connected directly to a machine.

1½ and 2-HP Single-stage collectors are better able to handle the cfm demands of a small central system. The Delta, Jet, and Penn State 1½-hp collectors provide the most cfm for the buck when compared to the 2-hp models. Having a large, 6-in. inlet dia. appears to be more important than horsepower when it comes to cfm performance. The 1½-hp can also run on any standard 20-amp household circuit while the 2-hp models need special wiring.

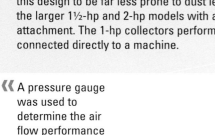

❮❮ A pressure gauge was used to determine the air flow performance of each machine in cubic feet per minute (cfm).

ART DIRECTION: JOEL SPIES · PHOTOGRAPHY: MIKE HABERMANN & BILL ZUEHLKE · ILLUSTRATION: FRANK ROHRBACH

CFM

Our chart includes two cfm readings; "Max" cfm and "Under Load" cfm.

To determine Max cfm we hooked up a 10-ft. section of maximum-diameter, smooth-walled duct to each machine and used clean bags.

Under Load cfm represents the real-world performance you can expect when the collector is hooked up to a small central system with bags that have developed a dust cake. Some collectors performed much better than others under these conditions.

The central system we set up for testing consisted of 20 ft. of maximum-diameter straight pipe, a 90-degree bend, all the appropriate step-downs and 6 ft. of 4-in. flex hose with a 90-degree bend. (We assumed the system would collect from one machine at a time.) A dust cake develops on all filters and bags as soon as they begin to collect dust. The dust cake actually improves filtering performance but it also cuts down on the airflow and thus the cfm of your machine. In addition to the effects of dust cake, the cfm performance of single-stage collectors drops another 20 percent as the lower bag gets full. (This is not true of cyclones.)

A Two-stage Cyclonic Collector

employs a cone-shaped canister to separate most of the debris before it reaches the impeller and filter. This makes removal of the dust and chips more efficient and convenient. Also, because the filter on a two-stage cyclone does not act as a container for chips, there is no subsequent drop in the cfm performance as the barrel fills with debris.

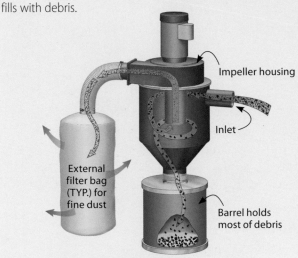

Impeller housing

Inlet

External filter bag (TYP.) for fine dust

Barrel holds most of debris

THE FILTER IS THE MAIN THING

The collection bags of single-stage collectors are expected to do double duty as filters. Unfortunately, most collector bags are made from woven fabric which is not particularly good at capturing fine particles (opposite, top left). The best bags are made from 16-ounce polyester felt which is a "rated" filter material designed to remove 99 percent of particles, 1 micron or larger (opposite, top right). But, this rating only holds true if one square foot of felt is used for every 10 cfm of airflow. In other words, if your collector is pulling 500 cfm, you need 50 sq. ft. of 16-ounce polyester felt.

The Penn State machines come closest to this ideal by using felt for both the top and bottom bags (32 sq. ft. for the DC2-5 and 22 sq. ft. for the DC1B-XL). (Aftermarket bags designed to handle 500 cfm are available from Oneida Air Systems; see Sources, page 132 and product review page 46.)

A few collectors get it half right with a felt top bag. But these collectors have a plastic bottom bag, which filters no air, leaks at the bag flange (see bottom) and is a nightmare to attach.

Of all the collectors that come with a felt bag(s), only Felder and Penn State use double or triple stitching on all seams. The others used single stitching to attach the round piece at the top of the bag. Single stitching can be stressed by the air pressure in the bag and open up escape routes for the dust-laden air. (See Sources, page 132, for suppliers of aftermarket bag upgrades with double stitching.)

Oneida Air Systems cyclone collector is unique in that it uses a pleated filter cartridge instead of a bag. The cartridge is made of non-woven, spun-bonded polyester that outperforms even 16-ounce polyester felt.

IMPELLERS

The collectors we tested had impellers made of steel, cast aluminum and plastic. Aluminum and plastic impellers are safest because they won't produce sparks when struck by metal accidentally vacuumed into the collector. Fires started this way are rare, but be mindful that there is a risk.

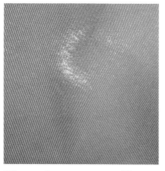

Woven bags are poor filters. The pinholes you see here allow the most hazardous fine dust to blow right back into your shop.

Felt filters are comprised of dense layers of polyester fibers, which trap most of the finest dust, while letting air pass back into the room.

Adjustable spring clamp

Attaching a collector bag after it has been removed for emptying is a fact of life with single-stage collectors. Getting the bag off isn't so tough, but putting it back on can be a real challenge. We found adjustable spring clamps provide the best combination of seal and ease of use for single-stage collectors.

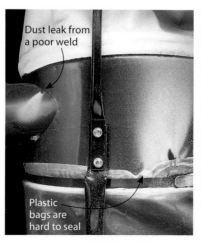

Dust leak from a poor weld

Plastic bags are hard to seal

Dust Leaks were common around bag flanges and duct welds. Plastic bags are a pain in the sitter to seal even when using spring clamps. Tip: A couple of 20-in. bicycle inner tubes can be stretched around the bag flange to help form a good seal for the bags. Silicone caulk can be used to seal any duct leaks.

Exhaust port

1 ½ HP american made motor

6" inlet

Internal pleated filter is easy to change—no bag required

Easy-to-handle barrel is included

Oneida Air Systems 1.5 HP Cyclonic Collector is clearly the best collector for a central dust collection system. It brings the superior engineering of industrial collectors to the small shop.

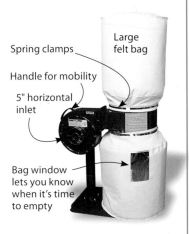

Spring clamps

Large felt bag

Handle for mobility

5" horizontal inlet

Bag window lets you know when it's time to empty

Penn State Industries 1-HP, single-stage collector comes with 16-oz. felt bags, a 5-in. inlet, is powerful for its size and had no visible leaks.

DUST COLLECTORS

Brand / Model	Inlet Diameter	CFM Max.*	CFM Under Load	Bags and Filters Material	Bags and Filters Spring Clamps
1 HP					
Delta 50-840	4"	440	365	W	Y
General 10-010	4"	410	350	F/W	Y
Grizzly G1028	4"	515	410	W	N
Jet 650	4"	455	365	W	Y
Penn State DC1B-XL	5"	665	420	F	Y
Sears 29978	4"	410	350	W	Y
Sunhill UFO-90	4"	490	380	W	N
Woodtek 802-124	4"	455	330	W	Y
Single-stage 1½ HP					
Delta 50-850	6"	895	495	W	Y
Felder AF-10	4.5"	420	345	F/P	N
Jet DC-1100	6"	860	495	W	Y
Penn State DC2-5	6"	860	610	F	Y
PowerMatic 073	2-4"	560	290	W/P	Y
2 HP					
General 10-110	5"	825	515	F/P	Y
Grizzly G1029	5"	825	485	W	N
Jet DC-1200	6"	1025	555	W	Y
Kufo UFO-101	5"	790	485	W	N
Sunhill UFO 101	5"	790	515	W	N
Woodtek 805930	5"	770	455	W	Y
Cyclone 1½ HP					
Oneida Cyclone	6"	745	702	SB	NA
Penn State Tempest	5"	420	381	F	NA

Brand	Motors AMPS	Volts**	Size WxLxH	Impeller	Dust Leak	Comments
Delta	9/4.5	115/230	16" x 29" x 60"	Steel	N	Minimal setup.
General	7	115	16" x 29" x 60"	Alum.	Y	Includes handle for mobility; bag clamp sewn into bottom for easy attachment.
Grizzly	14/7	115/230	22" x 38" x 76"	Steel	Y	Steel-strap bag clamps make for a tight seal but require a screwdriver to adjust.
Jet	11/5.5	115/230	14" x 27" x 57"	Steel	Y	Bag clamps sewn into each bag for easy attachment; no inlet grate prevents clogging but exposes impeller to damage from large debris.
Penn State	16/8	115/230	17" x 29" x 59"	Steel	N	Large-size bags; convenient handle; window on bottom bag.
Sears	7	115	16" x 28" x 60"	Steel	Y	Quick-change bottom bag; small top bag; handle for mobility.
Sunhill	12/6	115/230	14" x 27"x 55"	Steel	Y	Cinch strap bag clamps don't seal well; no inlet grate prevents clogging but exposes impeller to damage from large debris.
Woodtek	16/8	115/230	15" x 29" x 60"	Alum.	N	Easy setup; well-sealed housing was leak-free.
Delta	12/6	115/230	21" x 37" x 83"	Steel	N	Easy setup; well-sealed housing was leak-free.
Felder	7.2	230	16" x 31" x 78"	Steel	Y	In-line casters don't swivel; designed for 5-in. flex hose attachment; loud; plastic bags are extremely difficult to attach.
Jet	11/5.5	115/230	22" x 36" x 79"	Steel	N	Easy setup; quick-change bottom bag.
Penn State	18/9	115/230	20" x 37" x 73"	Steel	Y	Quiet, incomplete manual led to difficult setup; window on bottom bag.
PowerMatic	15/7.5	115/230	18" x 33" x 73"	Steel	Y	Gaskets on bag housing create a good seal; incomplete manual led to difficult setup; handle for mobility; plastic bag is difficult to attach.
General	9	230	23" x 37" x 76"	Alum.	Y	Well-sealed, square metal duct between bag housing and impeller housing was leak-free; plastic bag is difficult to attach and leaked at attachment flange.
Grizzly	24/12	115/230	23" x 38" x 76"	Steel	Y	Steel strap bag clamps make for a tight seal but require a screwdriver to adjust; power cord is undersized for 115V application.
Jet	15	230	21" x 38" x 79"	Steel	N	Well-sealed housing was leak-free; manual not up to Jet's normal standards.
Kufo	12	230	23" x 38" x 76"	Plastic	Y	Easy setup.
Sunhill	24/12	115/230	23" x 38" x 77"	Steel	Y	Easy setup; power cord is undersized for 115V application.
Woodtek	24/12	115/2330	22" x 37" x 77"	Alum.	N	Easy setup; well-sealed housing was leak-free; power cord is undersized for 115V application.
Oneida	17.2/8.6	115/230	24" x 24" x 84"	Plastic	N	Quiet; includes barrel and fittings; mobile stand available; manual difficult to follow; comes without a power cord. Free central system design service.
Penn State	18/9	115/230	20" x 20" x 90"	Steel	Y	Quiet; good manual; does not include barrel; mounting bracket needs to be constructed by owner (requires one sheet of plywood).

* With clean bags and 10 ft. of straight pipe.
** Motor voltages vary from 110/220 to 220/240.

W=Woven fabric
F/P=Felt top/plastic bottom

F=Felt
SB=Spun-bonded filter media cartridge

By DAVE MUNKITTRICK

Cartridge Dust Filters

BETTER FILTRATION FOR SINGLE-STAGE COLLECTORS

The cartridge filter is the first significant improvement in single-stage dust collection in more than 30 years. Cartridge filters offer better filtration, better airflow, and easier cleaning than bag filters (right). They are available on new dust collectors or as a replacement for the old filter bag on your existing single-stage machine. The upgrade doesn't come cheap (approx $200 for the 20-in. cartridge). What's really amazing about these filters, however, is they pack five to six times the filter area into a cartridge that's smaller than the bag it replaces!

BETTER FILTRATION

The filter material in cartridge filters is made of spun-bond polyester, capable of filtering dust particles down to 2 microns. Compare that to a typical woven fabric bag filter that struggles to capture dust at 30 microns.

A disposable plastic collection bag replaces the lower bag, because the lower bag no longer needs to do double duty as a collection sack and a filter.

ENHANCED CFM

A single-cartridge filter offers much more filter area than a single-bag filter (photo, page 50). That's because the filter material is folded or pleated like an accordion. The pleated filter design fits a ton of filter material into a small package. The increased filter area makes it easier for air to flow through the filter. We did some testing on the 1½-hp single-stage collector in our shop and found that switching to a cartridge filter resulted in a 20-percent bump in cfm performance.

DUST-FREE FILTER CLEANING

Cleaning a bag filter often means transferring fine dust from the bag to your clothes, shop, and lungs. Cartridge filters put an end to that nonsense. There's no need to remove a cartridge filter from your collector to clean it. Jet and Penn State cartridge filters feature a set of offset paddles built into the filter (photo, page 50) that allow you to knock the dust cake off the pleats with a few turns of a crank.

All that nasty wood dust drops harmlessly into the plastic collection bag for easy disposal. This system keeps you, your shop, and lungs cleaner.

EASY INSTALLATION AND BAG CHANGES

The cartridge filters we tried were easy to install on older model single-stage collectors. Just drop them onto the bag flange where your upper filter bag normally goes. The foam gasket on the cartridge filter makes an airtight seal on the rim.

BETTER THAN AFTERMARKET BAGS

High-performance aftermarket bags cost less than a cartridge, and some claim to filter to 1 micron. The trouble is these bags are undersized and that means reduced cfm performance for your collector. Also, because the bags are too small for the amount of air being forced through them, a lot of dust gets pushed right through the bag and back into your shop.

You can get custom bags made to the correct size that cost about $120. That's almost the cost of a cartridge filter and you'd still be faced with the cleaning hassles inherent in any bag system.

COMING SOON

There are some brand-new cartridge filter systems in the pipeline for the coming year:

■ Delta is developing a new filtration system to replace their bags. Still in the research phase, this system may be completely different than the cartridge filters featured in this article.

■ Laguna is completely redesigning their line of cartridge-based dust collectors. Expect their release sometime soon.

■ SECO offers a complete line of dust collectors with cartridge filters. Plus, they have a new line of self-contained hybrid dust collectors that use cartridge filters and offer some of the benefits of a cyclone system without the space requirements.

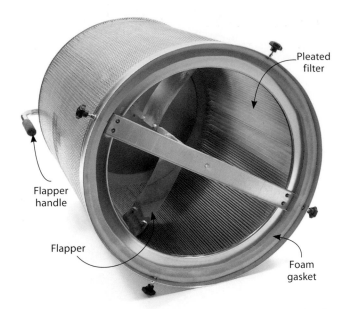

Pleated filter material offers increased airflow and better filtration than typical bag filters. A foam gasket creates an airtight seal on the collector-bag flange. No more hassles with leaky band-clamp seals. Flappers allow you to clean the pleats of dust build up without having to remove the cartridge.

Random-Orbit Filter Cleaner

I've had my canister-filter dust-collection system for about two years. It works great, but I figured out a new way to get it super clean.

Some high-end shop vacuums clean their filters using a built-in vibrator. I asked myself, "Why not adapt this idea?" The last time I emptied my dust collector, I cleaned the filter as recommended by the manufacturer by rotating the internal flappers two or three times. Then I removed the sandpaper from my random-orbit sander and placed a small piece of material cut from a nonslip router pad under the sander. I used the sander with very light pressure to vibrate the canister's top and sides. A lot more dust shook out of the filter in just a couple minutes.

—*Lou Bush*

Wide-Mouth Dust Collection

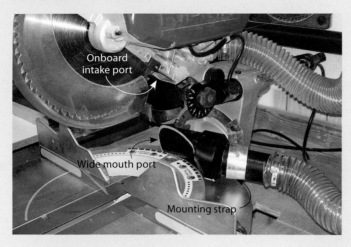

Onboard intake port

Wide mouth port

Mounting strap

The dust collection port on my sliding miter saw missed a lot of sawdust, so I added an additional port mounted directly behind the blade. The port is a piece of 3-in. ABS pipe that's cut at 45 degrees to create a wide mouth. The pipe is shaped to fit behind the saw's swiveling table, so it doesn't interfere with the table's operation. The port fits into a 3-in.-to-2-in. reducer and a wye-fitting connects hoses from both ports to my dust collection system. A strap anchored by one of the blade-tilt scale screws fastens the port to the saw. Now, instead of missing 90 percent of the dust, my saw captures almost all of it.

—*Perham Rogers*

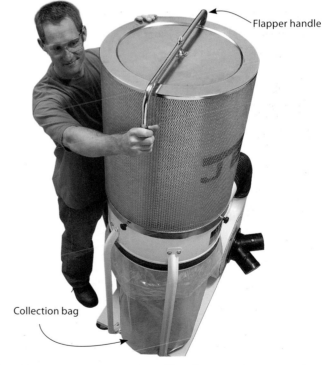

Flapper handle

Collection bag

Cartridge filters contain 5 to 6 times the filter area of a standard bag filter but they take up less space. The large filter area allows more air to pass through, which in turn increases the air-moving performance of your dust collector by about 20 percent.

Cartridge filters are easy to clean. There's no need to remove the cartridge. Just turn the handle and a pair of flappers (opposite, top) inside the cartridge knock the dust cake from the pleats. The fine dust from the filter drops harmlessly into the disposable collection bag below.

by DAVID MUNKITTRICK

Tool Test: Cyclone Dust Collectors

THE LATEST MODELS ARE BETTER AND CHEAPER THAN EVER

There has never been a better time to buy a cyclone dust collector. The new generation of cyclone machines is more powerful, more effective, more convenient—and less expensive. It is now possible to get a very fine 2-hp cyclone for less than $750. You can thank a competitive field and a growing demand from woodworkers for driving the innovations and prices.

For this test, we looked at all the 2-hp and 3-hp cyclones we could get our hands on. Many of these machines are newly designed. Some were so new the manufacturer couldn't get a stock model to us in time for testing.

Improving Airflow

A neutral-vane design smoothes the airstream inside a cyclone. The result is better airflow and more efficient separation of woodchips and dust from the air.

A neutral vane is basically an extension of the inlet tube into the cyclone body. Normally, the inlet tube is cut flush with the interior wall of the cyclone. As the air makes its first circuit around the cyclone, it smashes back into itself. That results in turbulence that, in turn, causes drag on the airflow.

Oneida's patented neutral-vane design (below, left) was the first on the block.

Grizzly's patent-pending internal air ramp (below, right) functions like a neutral vane. It directs the air stream downward as it enters the chamber.

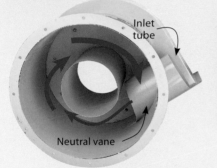
Inlet tube

Neutral vane

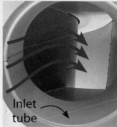
Inlet tube

《 A cyclone is a two-stage collector system that drops the debris out of the air flow before it filters the return air to the shop. It is more efficient and requires less maintenance than a single-stage collector.

ADVANTAGES OF A CYCLONE DUST COLLECTOR

Performance and Filtration

The cyclone is a two-step mechanical separator that, unlike a single-stage collector, drops solids from the air stream before they get to the impeller or filter. This allows the filter to run clean for long intervals. A clean filter allows greater airflow. Compare that to a single-stage collector in which the collection bag doubles as a filter and constricts airflow as the bag fills.

Because cyclone impellers handle relatively clean air, they can be designed to maximize airflow. A single-stage impeller, on the other hand, must be built to withstand the impact from debris; efficient airflow is secondary.

Cyclones tend to have larger impellers and inlets than single-stage collectors do. That makes cyclones better suited for central dust collection systems with large-diameter multiduct runs.

THE NEW-GENERATION CYCLONES

Boosting Performance

A cyclone collector is a deceptively simple-looking machine. Hidden inside the best machines is some clever engineering that enhances airflow and increases separation performance. Separation performance is simply a measure of how much debris falls out of the air stream into the collection barrel compared with the amount sent to the filter.

Neutral-Vane Design

The best-performing cyclones have what's called a neutral-vane design (see "Improving Airflow," previous page). Machines with a neutral-vane design seemed to push a whole lot less dust through their impellers and filters. This allows the use of highly efficient cartridge filters that would quickly plug with the dust sent through a machine without a neutral-vane design.

High-Efficiency Impellers

Backwardly inclined impellers (see photo, right) reduce noise and improve airflow and static pressure performance. A cyclone separates most of the debris before it hits the impeller, so manufacturers can use an impeller designed for maximum airflow. Not all manufacturers take advantage of this fact. Some use standard single-stage collector's impellers, which are designed for impact resistance as well as airflow.

Impellers with backwardly inclined fins move more air with less noise than straight-finned impellers do.

How a Cyclone Works

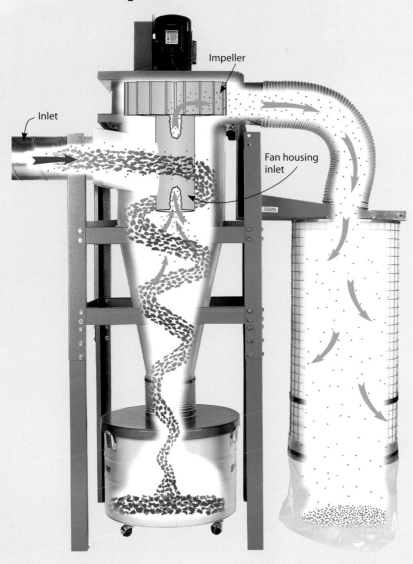

Inlet

Impeller

Fan housing inlet

A cyclone is a two-stage dust collector. During the first stage, the collection stream enters the cyclone at the inlet and debris is flung to the outside of the canister, where it spirals down into the collection drum, just like water draining out of your bathtub.

The fan-housing inlet tube begins the second stage. The tube hangs down in the middle of the cyclone body clear of the spiraling debris stream. The relatively clean air is pulled into the impeller, then pushed through the filter. The filter scrubs out the remaining fine particles. Dust that doesn't lodge in the filter media is collected in a separate bin, bag, or barrel beneath the filter.

Cartridge Filters and Shop Space

Cartridge filters not only do a better job of filtering the small stuff; they take up less shop space as well. The compact cartridge filter combined with a smaller drum allows manufacturers to build a cyclone that fits under an 8-ft. ceiling. That's really good news for basement or garage shop owners. Smaller drums are also a lot easier to manage when full.

Motors

A class F temperature-rated motor is best for a dust collector. A dust collector motor runs longer and works harder than any other tool in your shop. Whenever any tool is used, your dust collector is running. And unlike your tablesaw, it's under continuous load, so excessive heat can be a problem. Motors with an F temperature classification can really take the heat; they're rated to handle 311 degrees Fahrenheit. A class E motor has a lower temperature classification of 248 degrees Fahrenheit.

Recommendations

The 2- to 3-hp cyclone dust collectors we recommend are Oneida's Gorilla line and Grizzly's new generation of cyclones. Both manufacturers offer machines that incorporate a neutral-vane or similar design, cartridge filters, backwardly inclined impellers and class F motors. They both have high airflow performance. Very simply, they are fabulous machines at excellent prices.

We are also impressed with the new JDS cyclones and Penn State's new S series.

The best machines can ingest a barrel-load of sawdust and only leave a spoonful of very fine dust in the filter collector. The cyclones in our test that had the best separation performance all also had a neutral-vane design.

Airflow Test Results:

How Much Suction Do The Cyclones Have?

Judging how hard a dust collector sucks is more difficult than you might think. Horsepower of the motor doesn't tell you enough. The usual way of showing performance is with a fan curve, which shows the amount of air moved, in cubic feet per minute (CFM), as the static pressure in the ductwork increases. (You can think of static pressure as the resistance of your ductwork.) At a given static pressure, some machines will move more air than others will.

Unfortunately, there are several ways to measure the airflow and produce a fan curve, and manufacturers who provide this information often don't say how their tests were done. We tested dust collectors for this article using one commonly used approach and present the fan curves in the graph at top right. Fan curves available from manufacturers are presented at bottom right. They are sometimes quite different from ours, presumably because different testing methods were used or the machines have changed in the meantime.

Manufacturers are constantly working to improve their fan curves, and although CFM is important, designing your system to lower static pressure is just as important—and often neglected.

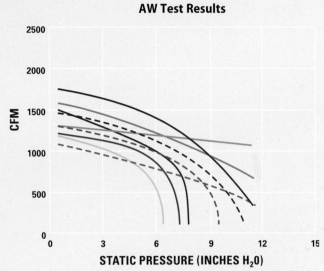

AW Test Results

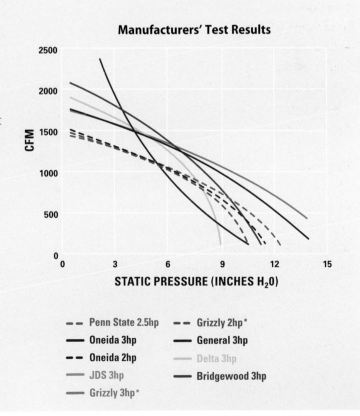

Manufacturers' Test Results

- - Penn State 2.5hp   - - Grizzly 2hp*
— Oneida 3hp   — General 3hp
- - Oneida 2hp   — Delta 3hp
— JDS 3hp   — Bridgewood 3hp
— Grizzly 3hp*

Oneida
2-HP DUST GORILLA
2-HP SUPER GORILLA
3-HP SUPER GORILLA

Oneida's specialty is cyclones. Dust collection is all the company does and cyclones are the only type of dust collectors it offers. Its new Gorilla line delivers top performance at a competitive price.

Separation in each model is excellent, with only a trace of dust ending up in the filter bin after the cyclone sucked up a barrel-load of shop dust. A high-quality pleated filter catches 99.9 percent of particles from 0.2 to 2 microns in size. Third-party filter ratings are available on Oneida's Web site, as is a host of other useful information.

Oneida's Super Gorilla line is the exact same cyclone as the Dust Gorilla with two upgrades: a U.S.-made Baldor motor and a higher-grade, longer-lasting filter material. The Super Gorillas and Dust Gorillas still have the same filter performance, because Oneida uses more square feet of the less-expensive filter media to make up the difference. All Oneida's filters can be cleaned by backwashing them with compressed air.

In addition to being backwardly inclined, Oneida's cast-aluminum impellers have airfoil-shaped fins for added airflow performance.

Oneida adds a foam silencer that greatly reduces exhaust noise. Its cyclones are still primarily made in the United States.

Height less than 8 ft.	✔
Neutral-vane design	✔
Cartridge filter	✔
Backwardly inclined impeller	✔

Pros
■ Free ductwork design is available from staff engineers.

■ Collection bin under filter seals well and is easy to take on and off. Plastic bags can be used in the bin for easy disposal.

■ Optional Bag Gripper ($140) allows use of a plastic bag in collection barrel.

■ Optional floor stand (shown), $160, has a small footprint.

Cons
■ No protective metal cage surrounds the Super Gorilla filter.

Grizzly

G0440, 2 HP
G0441, 3 HP

Grizzly has produced a really great line of cyclones. The icing on the cake is the built-in remote-control magnetic switch with timer. This convenience feature is worth more than $70 and is exclusive to the Grizzly cyclones.

The Grizzly cyclones have a ramped inlet design that acts like a neutral vane. As a result, they achieve excellent separation and airflow performance. A mere spoonful of fine dust enters the filter bag from each barrel-load of shop dust.

Grizzly's cartridge filter material captures 99.9 percent of particles 0.2 to 2 microns in size. Independent performance rating tests for the pleated filter material can be found on Grizzly's Web site.

Grizzly offers a built-in filter brush that moves up and down inside the filter like a chimney sweep's brush. This bonus feature makes filter cleaning convenient and fast.

Pros

■ Free ductwork design is available.

■ Remote-control magnetic switch is included.

■ Collection barrel rides on casters.

■ Sturdy metal floor stand is available (shown).

■ Gasket on filter bag flange prevents dust leaks.

Cons

■ Plastic bag on the filter is more cumbersome to take on and off than a bin would be.

Height less than 8 ft.	✔
Neutral-vane design	✔
Cartridge filter	✔
Backwardly inclined impeller	✔

JDS
2000CK, 2-HP
3000CK, 3 HP

The JDS cyclones are so new that we were only able to test the 3000CK.
Separation is good on the JDS. The 2 qt. of fine dust in the filter bag were far less than the gallons of dust in the some of the other cyclones' filter bags.

The JDS comes with a plastic bag to collect under the cyclone. An interior metal frame fits inside the bag and keeps it from being sucked into the cyclone. Bags are a real boon for people who put their wood dust out with the trash.

Height less than 8 ft.	✔
Neutral-vane design	
Cartridge filter	✔
Backwardly inclined impeller	NA

Pros
- You can use plastic collection bags under the cyclone.
- The 2-hp unit is only 6 ft. tall.

Cons
- Getting the frame out of a full 55-gal. bag of dust takes some twisting and tugging.

Penn State
1425S, 2½ HP
1535S, 3.5 HP

With the new S series, Penn State Industries continues to make significant improvements to its line of cyclones. The 1425S we tested had excellent separation, with only a trace of dust remaining in the filter bins. In the higher static pressure range, its airflow performance was better than than that of many 3-hp models. Penn State's cartridge filter is free standing. The filter collection bin cannot be removed for clean-out. Instead, a blast gate is set in the bin so you can vacuum out the bin. For this to work well, you'll need to have a high-quality shop vacuum that won't send all that fine dust back into your shop.

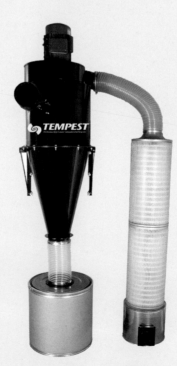

Height less than 8 ft.	✔
Neutral-vane design	✔
Cartridge filter	✔
Backwardly inclined impeller	

Pros
- Free duct design service is available.

Cons
- Filter bin clean-out is awkward.

Delta

50-901, 3-HP

The Delta is by far the quietest machine we tested and it's built like a tank. The 50-901 uses an acceptable filter bag, although it's not as efficient as a felt bag. The Delta comes with its own, sturdy tripod floor stand, but you must provide a drum for both the cyclone and filter. The Delta is primarily made in the United States.

Pros
■ Quietest cyclone in our test.

Cons
■ Height is high.

■ You must wire in your own switch.

Height less than 8 ft.	
Neutral-vane design	
Cartridge filter	
Backwardly inclined impeller	

General International

10-810, 3 HP,

We tested the General cyclone with the basic bag filter. We strongly recommend going for the cartridge filter, because the dust literally blew through the thin, woven fabric filter.

Height less than 8 ft.	✔
Neutral-vane design	
Cartridge filter	Opt.
Backwardly inclined impeller	✔

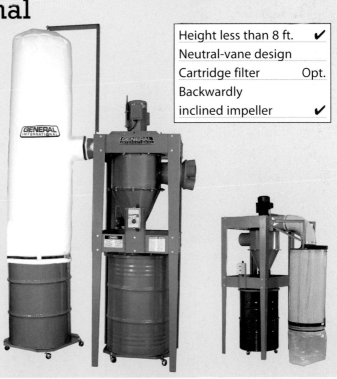

Pros
■ This model holds a 55-gal. collection drum and still fits under an 8-ft. ceiling.

■ Drum dollies are included.

Cons
■ Bag filter is a real dust spewer.

by WILLIS BOWMAN

Remote Control for your Dust Collector

A central dust collector is great, but having to walk across your shop to turn it on and off can be a real pain. Here's my ingenious solution: a remote low-voltage on-off switch near each blast gate. The switches turn on or off a relay, which lets power flow (or cuts power) to your dust collector. The switches are wired so you can turn the dust collector on or off from any blast gate no matter if it has been left on from a previous machine. Unlike other homemade circuits, this one is designed to comply with national electrical codes.

This circuit was designed for dust collectors with 115VAC, 1½ hp (or smaller) motors only. This requires a separate 20A, 120V circuit from your main electrical panel. For dust collectors with motors larger than 1½ hp (see the label on your dust collector motor) or if you are uncomfortable with wiring, contact a licensed electrician. In any case, we recommend that a licensed electrician make the final connection to your main electrical panel and inspect your connections.

Remote switch

Weather-proof switch cover seals out dust (standard switch is underneath cover)

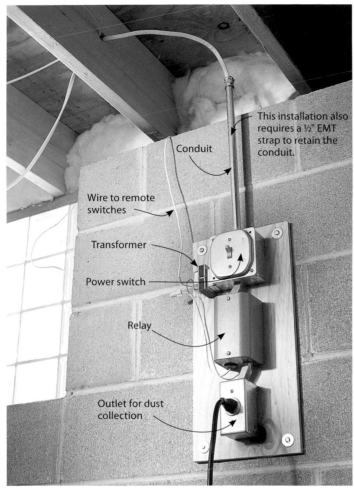

This installation also requires a ½" EMT strap to retain the conduit.

Conduit

Wire to remote switches

Transformer

Power switch

Relay

Outlet for dust collection

Low-voltage switches control a relay that switches the collector on and off.

« A remote low-voltage switch allows you to turn the collector motor on or off from any blast gate—a real convenience in a crowded workshop.

WHAT YOU'LL NEED

For one-stop shopping we've listed a Grainger stock number for all parts you'll need (see page 65). Call (800) 328-8010 to ask for the nearest Grainger outlet or visit www.grainger.com. You'll have to use a business name to place a phone or online order. Parts ordered from Grainger will cost about $150, but you can find many of these items at any home center for less.

STEP-BY-STEP INSTRUCTIONS

Having all your pieces in front of you is your key to success. First mount the transformer (F) on the side of the box (B) and mount the switching relay (L) inside the metal box (K). Next connect the three metal boxes (B, K and N) using the offset nipples (M) and line up the boxes as straight as you can. Mount the three connected boxes onto a 9 in. by 19 in. by ½-in. piece of plywood using wood screws.

Mount the plywood piece with the boxes onto the wall near both your electrical panel and your dust collector. Make sure the plywood gets screwed into a stud or concrete block. You can use drywall screws into studs or insert plastic anchors into cinder blocks and fasten with the recommended screws.

REMOTE CONTROL CIRCUITRY FOR DUST COLLECTION

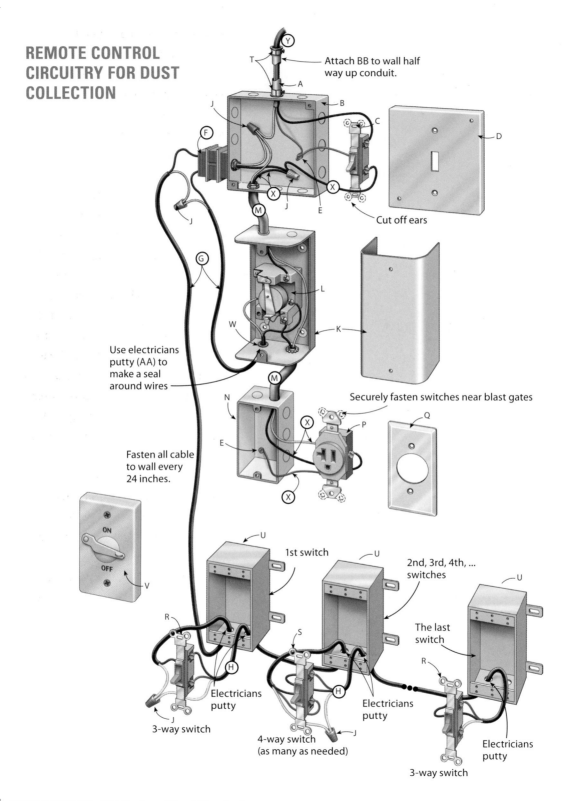

Attach BB to wall half way up conduit.

Cut off ears

Use electricians putty (AA) to make a seal around wires

Securely fasten switches near blast gates

Fasten all cable to wall every 24 inches.

ON
OFF

1st switch

2nd, 3rd, 4th, ... switches

The last switch

Electricians putty

3-way switch

Electricians putty

4-way switch (as many as needed)

Electricians putty

3-way switch

SUPPLY LIST

Reference	Quantity	Grainger Part Number	Description
A	1	6XC30	10' piece of ½" metal conduit
B	1	5A052	4" sq. box, 2⅛" dp, ½" knockouts.
C	1	6A704	20A 120V toggle switch
D	1	6XC67	4" sq. ½" raised single switch cover
E	2	*	ground screw, #10-32
F	1	4X744	20VA transformer, 120VAC / 24VAC
G	1	3ZK70	18/2 thermostat cable
H	1	3ZK71	18/3 thermostat cable
J	1 bag	6X687	Yellow wire nut
K	1	4A079	Metal relay enclosure
L	1	3X744	SPDT 30A 1½ hp relay, 24 VAC coil
M	2	*	¾" offset nipple
N	1	4A239	2⅛"-deep utility box
P	1	5C363	20A 125V single outlet
Q	1	*	Metal utility cover for single receptacle
R	A/R	5A060	Residential 3-way switch
S	A/R	*	Residential 4-way switch
T	2	5XC12	½" EMT conduit connector
U	A/R	3KG83	Weatherproof box
V	A/R	*	Weatherproof switch cover
W	1	*	Rubber grommet
X	A/R	4W192 4W193 4W187	12 ga. solid or stranded wire, white and black
Y	A/R	1W674	12/2 with ground NM-B nonmetallic sheathed cable (Romex)
Z	1 bag	3KF16	½" cable staples
AA	*	Electrician's putty	
BB	1	6XC41	½" EMT strap

* Find at your local home center.

Cut a piece of the conduit (A) that reaches from the top box up into your rafters. Fasten the conduit to the top box with a connector (T), and to the wall with a conduit strap. Then fasten another connector on top of the conduit. Make all wiring connections.

Next, mount the utility boxes (U) near your blast gates. Run the thermostat cable (G) from the control panel through a knockout in your first switch. Now, using the other thermostat cable (H), run a path from the first switch to the second, the second to the third and so on until you've connected the last switch. Neatly stuff all the wires into the boxes and then push the switches and outlets into the boxes. Secure the switches and outlets to their boxes and place the matching switch covers over them. Place some electrician's putty (AA) in the knockouts where the wires enter the box to act as a dust barrier.

Turn off the master switch (C) and plug your dust collector into the receptacle (P). Switch on the master switch and try the control switches. Your dust collector should turn on and off using any control switch. If not, switch the power off at the main electrical panel and check your wiring.

Tool Solutions

A good shop vac, plus a central dust collection system, solves the problem, right? Not so fast: you've still got to get the dust and chips from your machine cutters into the system. That's where real woodshop ingenuity comes in, as you'll see in this section.

《 The base of a typical contractor-style table saw is a leaky contraption, not easy to draw the sawdust into your collector. The solution shown here fills in that awkward space with a box that catches all of the debris and funnels it into the collector system.

Dust Collection Tips

PRACTICAL SOLUTIONS FOR A CLEANER SHOP

VACUUM-ASSISTED BENCH

I got tired of hooking my bench tools to my shop vacuum. Now I simply plug their dust collection hoses into the bench. I drilled and routed a hole in the bench to house the 2½-in. PVC pipe and hexagonal 2½-in.-to-1¼-in. reducer that I bought at a home center. My shop vacuum's hose fits the pipe underneath the bench. Above the bench, I use a tapered adaptor to attach my tool hoses. This setup also makes it easy to keep my benchtop clean. I just turn on the vac and sweep all the crud into the hole.

—*Miles Clay*

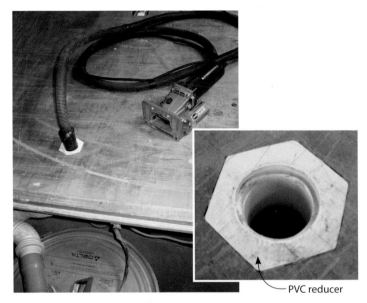

PVC reducer

HOSE CLAMP JIG

This T-track jig makes it easy to precisely position a dust collection hose on a router table or any other tool equipped with T-track. To make the jig, I cut a ½-in.-wide groove in a piece of ½-in. by 3-in.-square plywood to house a 2-in.-dia. reusable cable clamp (see Sources, page 132). The groove keeps the clamp from twisting. I attached the clamp with a No. 6-32 x ½-in. flathead machine screw. I recessed the nut in the bottom of the plywood, so it wouldn't interfere with the T-slot. Then I installed a ¼"-20 by 1-in. hex head bolt to slide the jig in the T-track and a wing nut to lock it in position.

—*Mark Thiel*

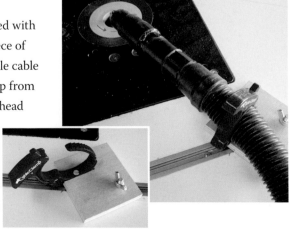

EDITOR: TIM JOHNSON • PHOTOGRAPHY: COURTESY OF THE CONTRIBUTER, UNLESS NOTED

USER-FRIENDLY DUST HOOD

The mounting bracket that came with the dust hood I purchased for my mini lathe was tough to adjust and difficult to remove. So I discarded it and designed my own, using a pair of ¾-in. by 2-in. by 10-in. oak rails and ½-in. rare earth magnets.

I fastened the magnet cups to the rails and then installed the magnets, positioned to rest on my lathe's bed. I drilled pilot holes before attaching the dust hood with sheet metal screws. I spaced the rails as widely as the hood allowed, to provide clearance for adjusting the tool rest.

—*Scott Muth*

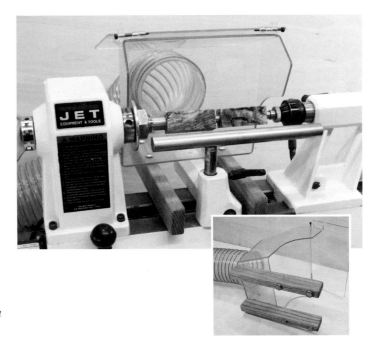

Economical Dust Collector Bags

My 1-hp. dust collector came with a plastic bag to collect the sawdust. The idea is to remove the bag when it's full, tie it off and dispose of it. Unfortunately, replacement bags cost $6 apiece. So I decided to substitute a heavy-duty 30-gal. trash bag. These bags don't cost much, about 45 cents apiece. However, they're made from thinner plastic than the factory bags, so I'm careful not to suck up nails or other sharp objects that might cause a puncture.

The bags are a little too wide, so I use tape to hold them in position while I lock the containment ring. The ring holds the bags firmly in place on the collector. When a bag gets full, I remove it, pull the drawstring closed, and set it out for the trash man.

—*Ira Penn*

Dovetail Jig Dust Collection

I created this device to capture dust and chips when I rout dovetails. The upholstery brush slides on the rod, so I can position it wherever it's needed. After gluing together an L-shaped plywood assembly, I cut a hole in the face and drilled a ¼-in.-dia. hole through the end. I ran a length of ¼-in. steel rod through the assembly and then bent both ends to fit around the lower knobs on my dovetail jig. Then I installed the upholstery brush, a common vacuum cleaner tool. The brush rests just below the jig's fingers, so it catches chips as they come off the router.

—*Mark Thiel*

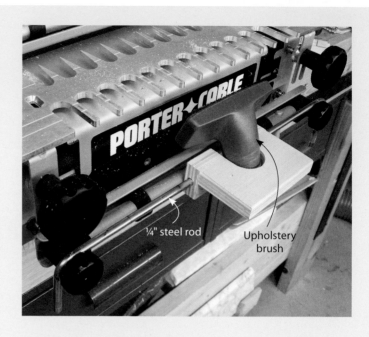

¼" steel rod   Upholstery brush

BLAST GATES FOR PVC DUCTWORK

For dust collection, my shop has PVC pipe buried in the dirt under the concrete floor. PVC is economical. But there's a catch: Nobody makes compatible blast gates. So I designed my own, using a pair of PVC water closet flanges.

I cut a U-shaped opening in a piece of ¾-in. MDF and sandwiched it between the flanges. Then I cut blast gates from ¾-in. plywood, one to block the air and one to allow it to flow. As ¾-in. plywood is thinner than ¾-in. MDF, the handles slide easily. I painted them red and green to indicate function.

I mounted the assembly on the floor pipe and attached the flexible hose. Now a quick glance tells me if the gate is open or closed.

—*Ray Merrell*

PVC closet Flange

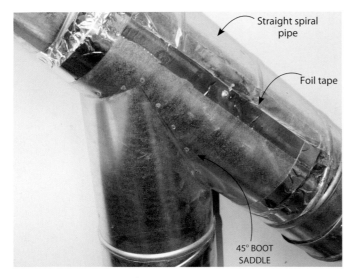

Straight spiral pipe

Foil tape

45° BOOT SADDLE

SHOP-MADE WYE FITTING

When I got my Cyclone dust collector, I decided to install spiral ductwork. But I was shocked when I saw the cost of the wye fittings.

Then I noticed 45-degree boot saddles, used to retrofit existing ductwork (see Source, page 132). I did the math and figured I could make my own wye fittings for less than half the cost of factory-made. I positioned the boot saddle where I wanted it to go on a straight run of spiral pipe and traced the inside opening, where the hole is to be cut out. After cutting the hole, I pop-riveted the boot saddle in place and used foil duct tape to seal it up.　　　　　—Rob Mousel

CHIP-FREE MORTISES

I use a low-tech setup to clear chips when I'm mortising. I simply tape my shop vacuum's hose on top of an old can that's filled with sand. A one-quart can puts the hose at the perfect height to remove chips directly from the bit's ejection port. The result is a cool-running bit and a chip-free mortise.

—Jeff Herman

Any-Which-Way Blower

The factory-supplied dust blower for my scroll saw wouldn't stay in position, so I replaced it with snap-loc coolant hose. Now I can position the hose anywhere I want it, including out of the way.

To attach the hose to the saw, I snapped on a connector and pressed it into a piece of ½-in. copper tube. The copper tube was a little large for the saw's blower fitting so I caulked the joint and tightened the tube down with a small machine screw.

—Mark Thiel

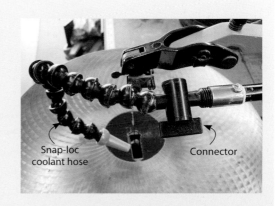

Snap-loc coolant hose

Connector

Panty-Hosed Vac

For years, my shop vacuum's best friend has been a discarded pair of panty hose. I cut a section from the upper part and slip it over the vac's pleated filter. The panty hose acts as a pre-filter, keeping out large particles that can quickly clog the pleated filter. Once the filter is clogged, a shop vacuum stops working, even if the canister is half-empty (photo at right). My panty hose pre-filter works so well that when the machine quits sucking up debris, I know the cannister is full.

—*Chuck Kubin*

MITER SAW DUST CATCHER

Before I built this containment box, my compound sliding miter saw spewed dust all over, even when it was connected to my dust collection system. Simply built from left-over materials, the box is designed to corral both airborne dust and sawdust sent behind the saw. It works very well. My box features a concave back that's shaped to match the saw's swing and baffles angled to accommodate 45-degree cuts. A curved top baffle completes the enclosure. Cleats hold these ¼-in. hardboard parts in position. A hose connected to the saw's port directs dust to the bottom of the box, which has a hole with an attached port to connect my shop vacuum's hose.

—*Todd Reimer*

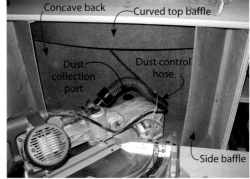

Concave back — Curved top baffle

Dust collection port

Dust control hose

Side baffle

⅛" hardboard back

Cleats

½" hardboard bottom

PLANER STOP-LEAK

The first time I used my new benchtop planer, its dust collection assembly leaked like a sieve. The snap-in-place exhaust port didn't seat properly, especially when the heavy dust collection hose was attached. Removing the exhaust port revealed more gaps in the dust collection's intake assembly.

To solve the problem, I removed the intake assembly and caulked all the mating surfaces. To seat the exhaust port firmly, while keeping it easy to install and remove, I tapped a pair of holes into the main casting and installed thumb screws.

—*Mark Thiel*

Intake assembly

Caulked joint

Tapped thumbscrew

Exhaust port

Low-Tech Air Scrubber

I turned an old box fan into an air scrubber by encasing it in a box with a pair of 20-in. by 20-in. furnace filters. I use an inexpensive filter on the infeed side to remove large particles. This filter fits loosely in its slot; when the fan runs, the airflow draws it tight against the fan. On the outfeed side, a 3M micro-allergen filter captures tiny particles. This filter fits its slot snugly, so dusty air can't escape. The fan runs constantly when I'm in my shop. I change the filters regularly, whenever I notice a decrease in air flow, and also at the end of every big project. A large dowel glued over the on-off switch makes the fan easier to turn on and off.

—*Rob Mousel*

Coarse filter

Fine filter

Air flow

Snag-free Hose

I love using dust collection with my orbital sander, but the hose always caught on the edge of my workbench. I fixed this problem by suspending the hose and cord using a 1-in.-wide cloth strap with some Velcro on the ends. One strap end is attached to a hook in the ceiling above my workbench. The other end loops around the dust hose and the power cord. I also made short sections of strapping to hold the power cord to the hose at a couple other spots. Cloth strap and Velcro are available at fabric or department stores.

—Peter Natoli

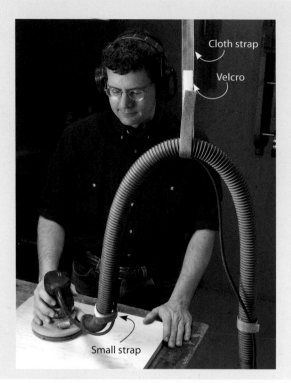

Cloth strap

Velcro

Small strap

Dust Sets Off Smoke Alarm

Q The smoke alarm in my basement shop keeps going off, apparently from dust. Can I get one that is set off by heat, or can tell smoke from wood dust so this doesn't happen? It's driving me nuts.

A In a word, no. You shouldn't use a heat-activated alarm as a substitute for a smoke alarm. These alarms don't give you the necessary warning. As you've discovered, smoke alarms are triggered by the particles in smoke and are set off just as easily by fine wood dust. The only solution is to control your airborne dust.

Thrifty Planer Collector

Wanna see a grown man cry? Watch him try to collect planer shavings with a small dust collector. The hose plugs up every time the shavings get caught on the metal grid across the collector's intake. Sawdust comes flying back out of the machine and covers the floor. Good grief!

If you've been through this, you may be tempted to throw away your 1-hp collector. Not so fast. Buy a special plastic lid and a standard 30-gal. metal trash can. (Use a metal can instead of plastic so you don't build up static electricity.) The lid turns the trash can into a "separator"—heavy planer and jointer chips fall into the trash can and are separated from the fine dust, which ends up in your collector's bags. The lid accepts conventional 4-in. hoses.

As a bonus, you've increased the capacity of your collector, because a 30-gal. trash can holds about twice as many shavings as the lower bag of a small collector. Your collector's impeller won't be damaged by flying pine knots. And you won't have to fiddle with unruly bag straps to dump out the chips. The separator lid simply lifts off.

Maximize the efficiency of your new two-stage system by using short hoses bent into wide arcs. First, place the planer directly over the trash can. Then, cut the trash can's original metal lid in half with tin snips and screw the semi-circular halves together to make a perfect hose support.

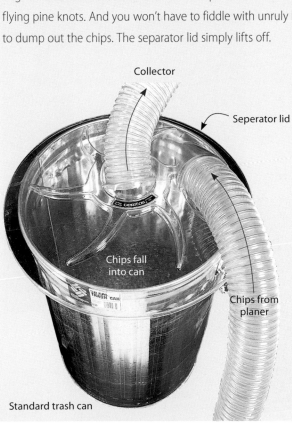

Collector

Seperator lid

Chips fall into can

Chips from planer

Standard trash can

BUST SANDER DUST AT THE SOURCE

Sanders kick out a ton of nasty dust. They make clouds of the fine stuff that ends up coating every surface in your shop. Your misery will be history, however, when you hook up a vacuum to your random-orbit sander. That layer of dust will be gone and your shop will never be the same.

Here's a hot setup that's mighty convenient to use: Plug your sander into a shop vacuum that has a tool-actuated switch. The vacuum comes on when you turn the sander on, and continues about 15 seconds after you turn the sander off. It's like having a remote control right on the sander. Twist a piece of 14-gauge electrical wire around the hose and cord so they don't get tangled up.

Most of the dust that used to fill your shop now goes directly into the vacuum, but continue to wear a dust mask—nothing's perfect!

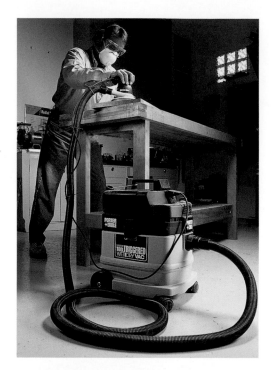

BAG THAT DUST

Don't you just hate it when you empty out your shop vacuum and poof—you're covered with dust again? I tried putting a garbage bag into my shop-vacuum. Whoops! It got sucked right into the vacuum's filter with all the dust.

Here's a simple but clever reusable plastic liner to the rescue. It expands to fit any size container and keeps the bag in place. Remove the liner before you tie up and pull the bag out of the vacuum.

LATHE DUST HOOD

Why be a dust-bowl refugee? Sanding on a lathe makes a storm of dust that can really irritate your nose and lungs, especially if it comes from spalted or exotic wood. Funnel that obnoxious stuff into your collector with this shop-made system. It uses flexible metal hose that stays put without clamps, so you can easily aim the funnel right at the dust source.

Make the funnel from a 10-in.-dia. aluminum light shield. You can find one at any hardware store for about $5. Remove the cord and socket and you've got a funnel with a small hole at the base.

The trick is to enlarge the hole to the size of your collector's hose. No problem. Use the same technique as you would for turning the bottom of a bowl or plate. Hold the light shield in a rim chuck made of solid wood or plywood. Fine-tune the groove of the rim chuck with a parting tool until the shield fits snugly within it. If the groove is too large in diameter, just make it a bit deeper and smaller. Add tape for insurance.

Now cut out the hole. Set your lathe to its lowest speed and score the thin aluminum shield with the point of your skew chisel. It will cut through in no time. Wear a heavy leather glove for protection. Voila! A 4-in. hole. Now insert aluminum dryer vent hose into the shield (about $1 for one foot).

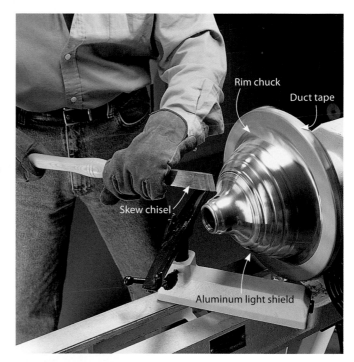

Rim chuck

Duct tape

Skew chisel

Aluminum light shield

Flexible dryer vent hose

Drum Sander Dust Collector

Suck up the fine dust that flies off a sanding drum with this simple setup. All you need is your shop vacuum, a 3-in. by 2-in. PVC reducing coupling ($1.35) and a pot magnet ($4). Bolt the magnet to the coupling and put the coupling over the end of the vacuum hose. A 2¼-in. dia. shop vacuum hose fits snugly inside the coupling's smaller end without clamps or glue. You can use this magnetic dust hood on any power tool with a metal table.

DRESS FOR DUST

Do the clothes really make the man? Try taking a tip from turners and dress up for dust. Wear a jumpsuit and a face shield when you can't collect sawdust at the source.

This is the outfit turners wear when they're making lots of chips. A jumpsuit is easy to brush off when you're done because it doesn't have any nooks or crannies for dust to get caught in. You can leave your dusty jumpsuit right in the shop.

The face shield is more effective than many safety glasses for keeping dust from getting in your eyes at a critical moment. It's also a first line of defense against breathing in sawdust, but remember to wear a dust mask as well.

TABLESAW DUST TRAP

Trap dust under your tablesaw before it spreads all over your shop! This cradle directs all that dust right into your shop vacuum hose.

Make a wood frame with two curved sides and two straight sides to fit the opening at the bottom of your saw, as shown. Your saw frame may not look exactly like ours, so customize the frame to fit. With tin snips, cut a thin sheet of galvanized steel ($3 for a 16-in. by 30-in. sheet at any home center) to fit your frame. Next, cut a 2½-in. hole in the center of the trimmed sheet with your snips.

To make the small wood connector that accepts the hose, glue together two 4-in. by 4-in. pieces of ¾-in. MDF or plywood and drill a 2½-in. hole in the middle. Add a 3-in. by 3-in. square of plywood to the bottom of the block and drill another 2½-in. hole to act as a tight-fitting collar. Shape the top face of the block with a belt sander or bandsaw to conform to the curve of the cradle. Connect the block to the steel by driving sheet metal screws through the inside of the cradle and into the wood block. Glue a hose connector in the hole with epoxy. Bolt the dust trap to the saw frame and hook up your shop vacuum.

Router Dust Hood

Have you ever used a router on MDF? Man, those dust plumes can rival the explosion of Mount St. Helens!

If you own a Porter-Cable router, here's an answer. It's an integrated sub-base and hood that practically collects all the dust right at the source, whether you're shaping an edge or plunging into a mortise. One nozzle collects from above, another from below. Standard 1½-in.-dia. hose fits both nozzles. We've used one in our shop, and though not perfect, it helps enormously in keeping down the dust.

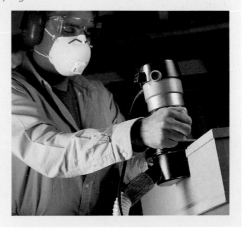

MAKE SHAVINGS, NOT DUST

Many woodworkers hate sanding. Even with dust collection, machine sanding is noisy and makes your arm feel like jelly. One good alternative is the scraper, a quiet hand tool that doesn't make any dust at all.

Think of a scraper as a substitute for sandpaper. In fact, scraping is faster than sanding. It's easy to remove mill marks with a Stanley #80 and get a perfectly flat surface to boot. Then turn to a plain cabinet scraper for the final licks. Your arms will get a healthy workout, but you won't have to worry about spewing dust into the air.

The harder the wood, the better the scraper will work. Lightweight woods, like pine and basswood, can't stand up to scraping, but with the majority of hardwoods you'll get a surface that requires only a very light sanding with fine paper.

Stanley #80 scraper

Cabinet scraper

THIN KERF RIP BLADE

It's hard to collect dust from a tablesaw, but choosing the right blade can help minimize the amount of dust you create. A thin-kerf blade makes about 25-percent less dust than a standard blade. That's far less dust in your face!

Here's more: Use a dedicated rip blade when cutting the length of a board. A rip blade makes relatively large shavings that are less harmful to your lungs than some of the small shavings and dust made by combination or crosscut blades. Combine rip teeth and a thin kerf into a single package and you've got a great dust-busting tablesaw blade.

A BETTER DUST MASK

All disposable dust masks are not created equal. The National Institute of Occupational Safety and Health (NIOSH) is looking out for you, so they rate masks for effectiveness. To keep your lungs healthy, look for the NIOSH-approved label on the box. These masks cost a bit more than the inferior "comfort" masks, but they're well worth it.

The healthier masks are made from finer filter material than the cheaper masks and are built to fit good and tight on your face. They have two straps rather than one and a metal band that you pinch to conform to the bridge of your nose. The best model has a valve in the center that opens when you exhale. This keeps the seal intact between your face and the mask. No more fogged up glasses.

Zero Clearance Dust Port

Zero clearance inserts are wonderful for eliminating tearout, but, unfortunately, they also impede dust collection. To give my collection system an opening to pull sawdust through, I cut a ½-in.-dia. hole at the front end of the blade slot. In this location, the hole doesn't adversely affect the benefits of my zero clearance insert.

—*Mark Thiel*

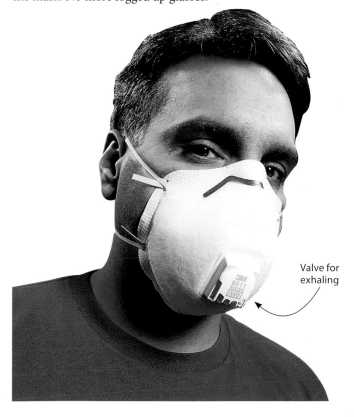

Valve for exhaling

by DAVID OLSON

Dust-free Bandsaw

SHOP-BUILT SHROUD REPLACES TINY PORT

I replaced my bandsaw's wimpy 1½-in. dust-collection port with a shop-made shroud that makes bandsawing virtually dust-free. The secret: My shroud's intake port is much larger (see photo and exploded view, at right). Another great feature is that the big hose mounts on the back, so it's out of the way.

I built this shroud by improving a similar design I'd seen in an old woodworking magazine. My shroud is mounted on a steel plate that I cut to size with my angle grinder (¼-in.-thick plywood would also work for the mounting plate). I attached this plate to the saw's casting, using the same tapped holes that held the original port. On saws without a port, you'll have to drill and tap a couple holes in the casting.

The shroud's angled top allows the table to tilt. I sawed the back plywood face to match the profile of the saw. I left the front face as wide as possible. It actually extends inside the door and is cut to fit around the wheel.

I cut a 4-in.-dia. hole in the back face and installed the sheet-metal duct. Then I attached the faces together with a length of 22-gauge galvanized sheet metal. The lip at the bottom helps keep sawdust in the shroud.

Once the shroud was mounted, I marked and cut the saw's lower door, so it would close. I was reluctant to alter my saw by cutting the door, but I'm glad I did. This shroud makes bandsawing much cleaner and more enjoyable.

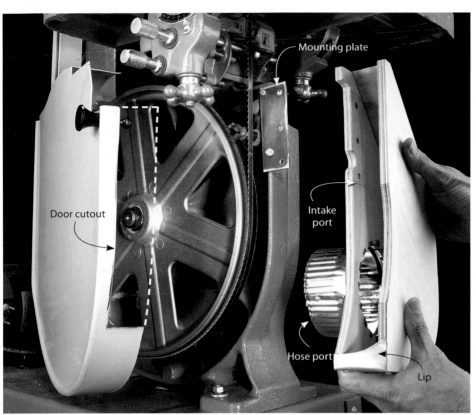

Mounting plate

Door cutout

Intake port

Hose port

Lip

The intake port is about the same size as the hose port, so it doesn't restrict the flow of air to the dust collector.

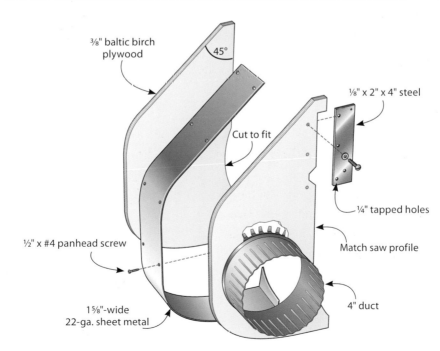

3⁄8" baltic birch plywood

45°

1⁄8" x 2" x 4" steel

Cut to fit

1⁄4" tapped holes

Match saw profile

1⁄2" x #4 panhead screw

15⁄8"-wide 22-ga. sheet metal

4" duct

by WAYNE HORNE

Anti-Slip Dust-Collection Table

PERFORATED TABLE TOP SUCKS DUST DOWNWARD

Here's a pair of sanding helpers that work great together. The rug pad provides a soft anti-slip surface. The pegboard, combined with the holes in the rug pad, allows dust to be sucked down through the table. My shop vacuum provides plenty of airflow.

I bought the wood for my sanding table at the local home center for about $20. I found the anti-slip rug pad at the same store in the carpet department for $6. The pad was bigger than my table, but was easily cut to size with a scissors.

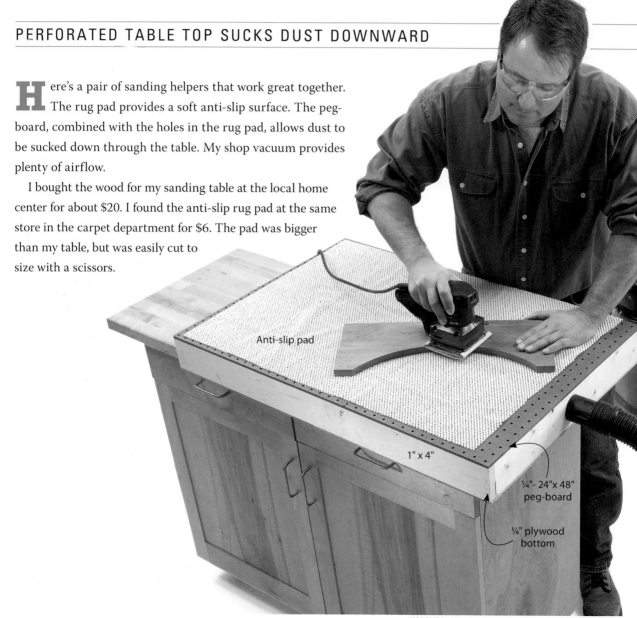

Anti-slip pad

1" x 4"

¼"- 24"x 48" peg-board

¼" plywood bottom

ART DIRECTION: VERN JOHNSON • LEAD PHOTO: BILL ZUEHLKE; ALL OTHERS, STAFF

Dust Collection for Routers

REMOVE THE DUST AT THE SOURCE

Q I'm sensitive to wood dust, so I'd like to reduce the amount of dust my router throws. What are my options?

—*Drew Klassman*

A The best way to fight dust is to remove it right at the source. Collecting dust is fairly easy with a dust hood on a router table, but trapping and sucking up the dust from a moving router is no picnic.

Routers can shoot dust in two completely different directions. When you cut grooves or mortises or do inlay work, for example, all the dust shoots up and out the sides of the router. But when you cut a profile on the edge of a board or use a flush-trim bit, most of the dust flies out below the router. The trick is to find a way to collect dust from both above and below the baseplate.

Router manufacturers haven't yet come up with the perfect solution. At right, you'll find some of the best ideas on the market. In general, plunge routers are better equipped than fixed-base routers.

A built-in dust collection system for mortising and grooving is mighty convenient. You'll find this feature on DeWalt, Festo and Black & Decker plunge routers. DeWalt also makes an edge guide with a dust-collection port.

Inexpensive ($10 to $15) dust-collection accessories sold by many plunge router manufacturers are not quite as effective at capturing dust. Also, their molded plastic edges may obscure your view of the bit.

This nozzle attachment, from Leigh, is perfectly suited for use on a dovetail jig, but only somewhat effective for edge work. It fits most routers. For maximum efficiency, you can position the nozzle very close to the bit. Unfortunately, you can't use this attachment and an edge guide at the same time because the attachment fits into one of the edge-guide holes.

Removable basket

This accessory baseplate for Porter-Cable routers collects the dust made by almost every kind of router operation. Once attached to your router, it's virtually a built-in system. You can use an edge guide with it, also.

ART DIRECTION: PATRICK HUNTER • PHOTOGRAPHY: STAFF, UNLESS OTHERWISE INDICATED • ILLUS

by KEVIN GROENKE

Handy Blast Gate Lever

OPERATES WITH A SIMPLE PUSH AND PULL

Reaching down to open and close my tablesaw's blast gate was a real pain until I built this pivoting mechanical arm from pieces of ⅛-in. flat steel and ⅜-in. rod. It may look cobbled together, but it works great.

I drilled holes, fastened the linkages with nuts, bolts, and washers, and attached the wooden handle. Now the gate operates by a simple push or pull.

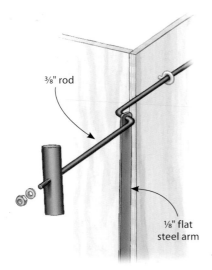

⅜" rod

⅛" flat steel arm

An S-shaped bend in the rod captures the arm.

EDITOR: TIM JOHNSON • ART DIRECTION: RICK DUPRE • PHOTOGRAPHY: RAMON MORENO, UNLESS OTHERWISE INDICATED • ILLUSTRATION: FRANK ROHRBACH

by MARK NEGAL

Capture Tablesaw Dust

ANGLED BOX CLOSES THE BASE

EDITOR: TIM JOHNSON • ART DIRECTION: VERN JOHNSON • PHOTOGRAPHY: PATRICK HUNTER

My contractor-style tablesaw spewed sawdust everywhere until I enclosed the base by covering all the openings with ¼-in. MDF panels. First, I added two aluminum angle rails so the collection box slopes toward the dust port in the back panel. Then I screwed on the MDF panels.

I made two custom-fit panels to cover the open back, one for 45-degree cuts and another for 90-degrees cuts, because those are the most common blade positions I use. These panels rest on the lip at the back of the opening and simply slide in and out of place. I marked them for cutting by measuring around the motor mount and belt guard.

Milk Jug Dust Collection

Routing makes a real mess. But, here's a solution that won't cost you a dime. Take a 1-gallon milk or windshield-washer container and cut a hole in one side for a bit. Slice off the bottom with a utility knife. Cut back the three other sides so they line up with the centerline of your router shaft. Push a 1-in. vacuum hose onto the neck of the jug, fire up the vacuum and rout to your heart's content without having to sweep up afterward.

—*Spike Carlsen*

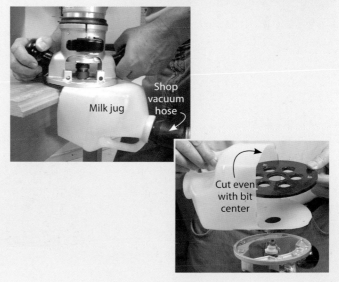

Milk jug

Shop vacuum hose

Cut even with bit center

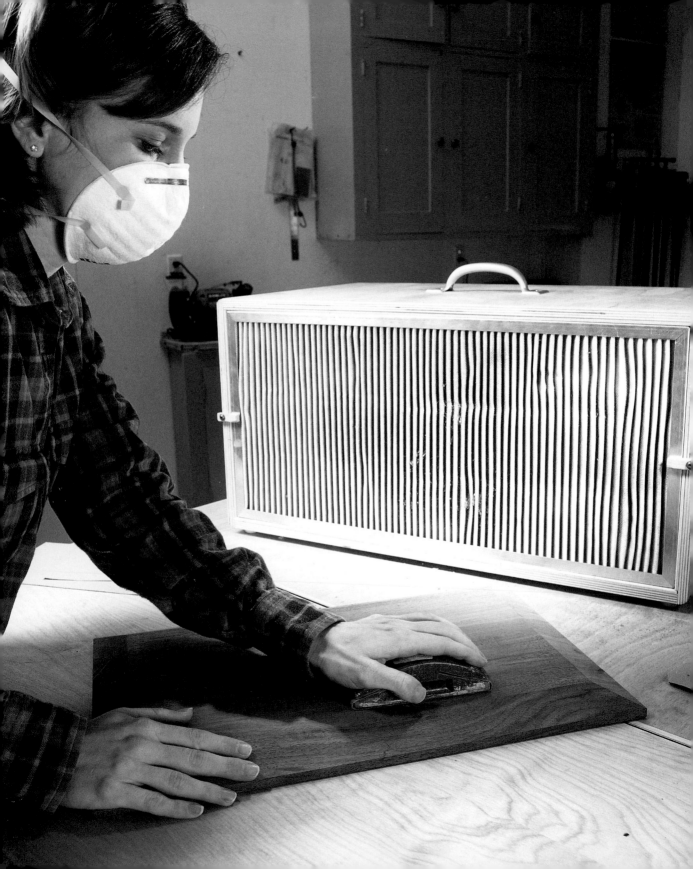

Clean the Air

Vacuum up the shavings, collect the dust and chips as they emerge from machine cutters, and you're still left with tiny particles wafting through the workshop air and into your lungs. The next step in dust control is to install a filter system to clean all the air in the workshop. It's easier and simpler and a lot more effective than you might imagine.

« This portable, shop-built air scrubber catches most of the airborne fine dust from hand-sanding.

JDS AIR-TECH 2000
HIGH EFFICIENCY AIR FILTRATION SYSTEM
THE JDS COMPANY   COLUMBIA, S.C.

by DAVE MUNKITTRICK

Tool Test:
Shop Air Cleaners

TAKE DUST CONTROL TO THE NEXT LEVEL

Gone are the days when a dusty shop was considered a productive shop. Now, a dusty shop is a hazardous shop. Fine dust makes a mess of everything, including your lungs. Due to this heightened awareness, dust collection has become a fast-growing area for manufacturers of woodworking equipment. Air cleaners are designed to hang from the ceiling where they can reduce the amount of fine dust suspended in your shop's air.

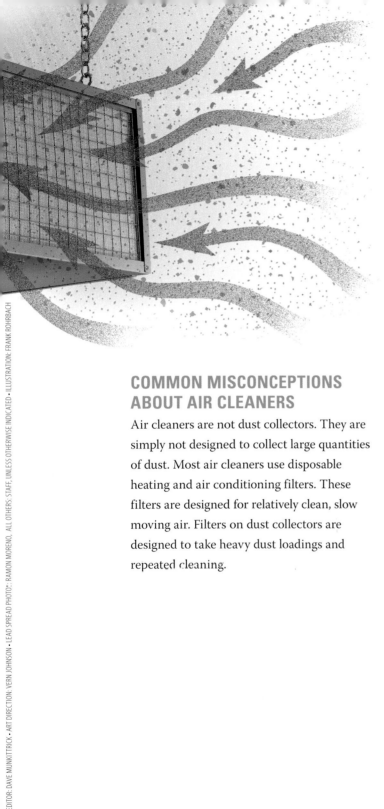

EDITOR: DAVE MUNKITTRICK • ART DIRECTION: VERN JOHNSON • LEAD SPREAD PHOTO: RAMON MORENO, ALL OTHERS: STAFF, UNLESS OTHERWISE INDICATED • ILLUSTRATION: FRANK ROHRBACH

DON'T PUT THE CART BEFORE THE HORSE

Before rushing out to buy an air cleaner, get a high-quality dust collector with proper filters first. Add a shop vacuum to collect from your hand-held power tools. Together, these two systems will capture the vast majority of the dust your shop produces. An air cleaner will help capture the fugitive dust that escapes your other systems.

THE BALANCE OF AIR FLOW AND FILTRATION

Effective air cleaning is a race against time. Once a dust particle becomes airborne, it's only a matter of time before it settles in your shop or lungs. To get the dust before it can settle, an air cleaner must circulate all the air in your shop every six minutes.

So, lots of airflow, measured in cubic feet per minute (cfm), is a good thing. But the cfm capacity of an air cleaner is only half the equation. You also need a top-notch filter to capture the fine dust. Only a few of the machines in our test successfully combined good cfm and good filtration.

Some machines have great filters but are less than robust in the cfm department. Others had lots of airflow but less efficient filters.

COMMON MISCONCEPTIONS ABOUT AIR CLEANERS

Air cleaners are not dust collectors. They are simply not designed to collect large quantities of dust. Most air cleaners use disposable heating and air conditioning filters. These filters are designed for relatively clean, slow moving air. Filters on dust collectors are designed to take heavy dust loadings and repeated cleaning.

TESTING AIR CLEANERS

Because of the technical expertise required to accurately test air filters, we took all the cleaners to Particle Tech, Inc., a professional testing lab in Minneapolis. Before the test we installed self-stick weather strip on the filter flanges of each machine to reduce leaks. Each machine was set in a sealed test chamber where a total of 80 grams of standardized test dust was introduced in 16-gram increments called "loadings." The standardized dust we used was made up of particles that ranged in size from 100 microns to less than 1 micron. Dust that got through the machines was captured and weighed to determine how much dust the air cleaner let through.

With each loading, cfm readings were also taken to track how the airflow degraded as the filter got dirty.

Dust collector

Mask

SHOP FOX

Vacuum

Air cleaners are the last line of defense in the war on wood dust. First comes a high-quality dust collector that captures the dust directly from your machines. Next comes a vacuum to capture the clouds of dust from your hand-held power tools. Finally, add an air cleaner to get what's left. Don't forget a dust mask to protect your lungs from the dust that's on its way to your air cleaner.

How Do They Work?

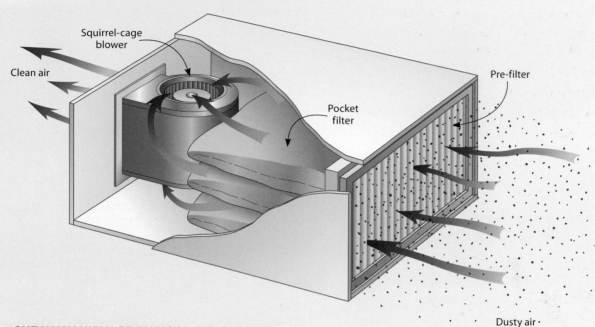

Squirrel-cage blower

Clean air

Pre-filter

Pocket filter

Dusty air

CUTAWAY VIEW OF TYPICAL AIR CLEANER

An air cleaner is simple in principle: a box with a squirrel-cage blower run by a small (fractional hp) electric motor. The blower pulls air through two or more filters, typically a pre-filter and a pocket filter. The pre-filter protects the more expensive pocket filter from getting prematurely plugged with debris. The pocket filter captures the finest particles.

The amount of air that passes through an air cleaner is measured in cubic feet per minute (cfm).

Balancing Air Flow with Filter Efficiency

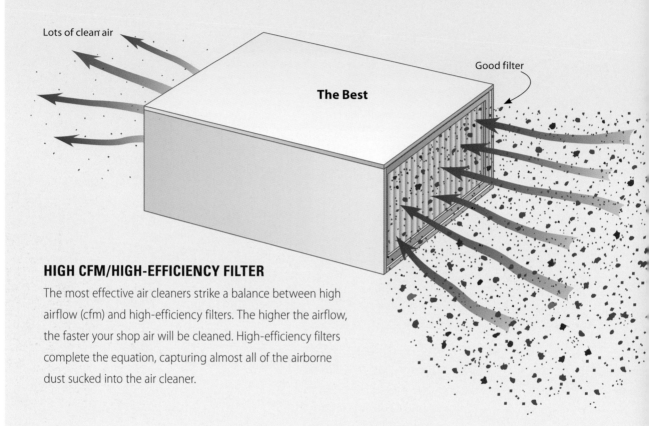

Lots of clean air

The Best

Good filter

HIGH CFM/HIGH-EFFICIENCY FILTER

The most effective air cleaners strike a balance between high airflow (cfm) and high-efficiency filters. The higher the airflow, the faster your shop air will be cleaned. High-efficiency filters complete the equation, capturing almost all of the airborne dust sucked into the air cleaner.

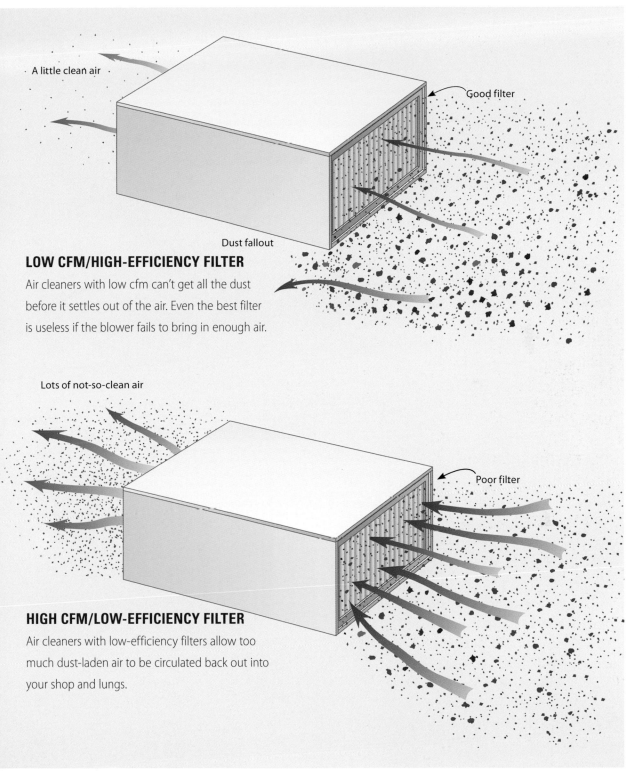

A little clean air

Good filter

Dust fallout

LOW CFM/HIGH-EFFICIENCY FILTER

Air cleaners with low cfm can't get all the dust
before it settles out of the air. Even the best filter
is useless if the blower fails to bring in enough air.

Lots of not-so-clean air

Poor filter

HIGH CFM/LOW-EFFICIENCY FILTER

Air cleaners with low-efficiency filters allow too
much dust-laden air to be circulated back out into
your shop and lungs.

FILTRATION

The "Blow Through" heading in the chart, page 100, tells you how many grams of the test dust got through each machine. It is a direct measure of filtration performance.

The blow through numbers are quite small, but keep in mind that this represents the smallest, most harmful particle sizes. So, a small difference in weight is actually a big difference in performance. For example, our worst performing machine let 68 times as much harmful dust through as our best performing machine. That's huge.

Manufacturers often use percentages to rate filter performance but this is misleading. In our test, the worst performer captured 91.5 percent of the dust and the best captured 99.875 percent. Long years of schooling have conditioned us to look on a 90 percent score as a great success. But that's just not the case with filtration.

REAL WORLD CFM

Avoid using the manufacturer's cfm numbers when comparing air cleaners. These are often based on the blower running without the filters installed. Not a very realistic number.

We took a total of six cfm readings on each machine, starting with clean filters and once for each 16-gram loading of test dust. As the filter loads with dust, the cfm decreases. The "Dirty Filter CFM" rating in the chart is the last reading taken after all 80 grams of dust have been run through the machine. The "Average CFM" in the chart represents the average of all six readings and is a good working number to use when determining what size machine you need for your shop.

WHAT SIZE AIR CLEANER DO I NEED?

As a rule of thumb, your air cleaner should filter all the air in your shop every six minutes. This is a minimum. An air cleaner that can do the job in less time is better because it will clean the contaminated air in your shop that much more quickly. To determine the size or how many cleaners you need, start by calculating the cubic feet of your shop (L x W x H). Divide that number by 6 and you'll have the minimum number of cubic feet per minute, or cfm, the air cleaner needs to pull through it's filters. Use the "Average CFM" number from the chart to see if the collector you're looking at is right for your shop space.

For example, if your shop measures 15 ft. x 20 ft. x 8 ft., it contains 2,400 cubic feet of air. Divide by 6 to get the minimum cfm required, in this case 400.

Air Cleaner Tips

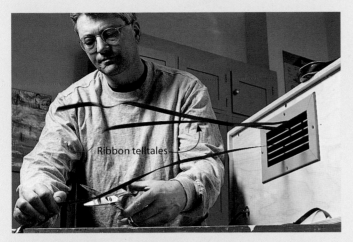

Ribbon telltales

TELLTALE FILTER MONITOR

Ribbons on the exhaust port are a visible cue that it's time to change your filters. With a clean filter installed, tie a few long ribbon "telltales" onto the exhaust grate. Then, turn on the machine and shorten them until they flutter horizontally. They'll begin to droop at about a 45-degree angle when it's time to change the filters.

WHERE TO LOCATE YOUR AIR CLEANER

Locate your machine as centrally as possible but cheat it toward areas where the dust is created. For example, a good location is over an assembly table where you do hand sanding.

For best results, especially in larger shops, buy two smaller units rather than one big one. That's because your air cleaner tends to pull hardest on the air around it leaving the far corners of your shop virtually untouched. Two cleaners can be set up to create a current around the shop to maximize the circulation of air through the machines.

Filter flange

Self-stick weather strip

PREVENT LEAKS

Add a gasket on the filter flange to prevent air from bypassing the filters. Some models come with a gasket on the filter flanges, but all the ones we saw were poorly installed, leaving large gaps. You can apply your own gaskets using self-stick weather strip available at hardware stores.

PRE-FILTERS

Air cleaner pre-filters are either disposable or washable (photos next page). The choice is yours. A disposable pre-filter will be replaced many times before the pocket filter behind it needs replacement. You may be tempted to vacuum off a disposable pre-filter, but don't. This can damage the fabric and reduce the filter's efficiency.

Washable pre-filters, on the other hand, offer convenience and long-term cost savings. When they get dirty, you simply rinse them out, let them dry and put them back into service. The money you save using a washable filter may get spent in more frequent pocket filter changes, however, because the washables let more dust through.

REMOTE CONTROL

A remote control may be important if your machine is going to be out of reach. On some machines the remote control is the only way to adjust speed or set the timer (a bad deal if you run out of batteries or lose your remote).

TIMER AND VARIABLE SPEEDS

A timer and/or variable speeds are available on some machines. Timers are great and allow the machine to keep cleaning your shop air when you're not there. Variable speeds allow you to run your machine at a lower cfm. This reduces the noise you have to put up with, but the lower cfm also reduces the effectiveness of your cleaner.

NOISE

These machines are running for long periods of time, so noise can be an issue. All the machines were relatively quiet (we're talking about a woodshop here). The trade-off for a quiet machine is lower cfm. You just can't have your cake and eat it, too.

Features

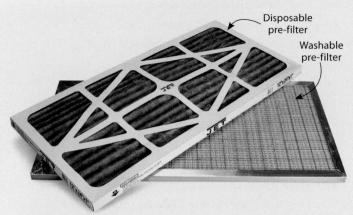

Disposable pre-filter

Washable pre-filter

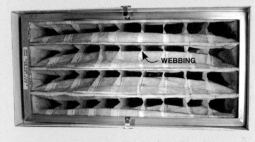

WEBBING

Disposable pre-filters do a better job than washable pre-filters. However, washable pre-filters offer greater convenience: simply wash clean with water, dry, and reuse.

Webbing or stitching is used on the best performing pocket filters, allowing the filter to open up like a parachute into the air stream. The webs also prevent the individual pockets from contacting each other for uniform airflow through the filters.

radio remote control

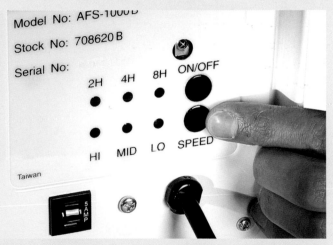

Remote controls let you operate your machine when it's out of reach. We liked radio-controlled remotes the best. They don't require you to aim the remote or have a clear shot at the control panel. They even come with key slots in the back so they can be hung on the wall.

Timers allow you to clean the air when you're not around. Just set the air cleaner to run a few hours after you're done and you'll return to a clean shop. Variable speeds are of less value. The machine is quieter on a low setting, but for best performance, it needs to be circulating as much air as possible.

RECOMMENDATIONS

Our picks represent the optimal combination of cfm and filtration. Units that allowed more than a gram of dust through were excluded from consideration. At first glance, this may seem overly restrictive, but a small difference in efficiency can make a huge difference in effectively capturing small, health-damaging dust particles.

Runners Up

A couple of models would have made Best Buy and Editors' Choice had filtering or cfm performance been better.

The Delta 50-875 was a top Editors' Choice contender. It has great filtration but about 11-percent less cfm than the Editors' Choice, the JDS 750-ER.

Jet put up some strong cfm numbers, but both Jet machines let more than twice as much dust through as the JDS 750-ER.

The General Int'l 10-550 comes with a remote and good cfm, all at a great price. It would have been a strong Best Buy candidate if it hadn't let through four times more dust than the Delta AP-200, our Best Buy. The same thing can be said for the Shop Fox: great cfm and good features, but it fell down on filtration. The Lee Valley 03J05.20 took top honors in filtration, but was weak on the cfm side.

AIR CLEANERS

Brand & Model	Phone Number	Clean Filter CFM/ Dirty Filter CFM	Average CFM	Blow Though (in grams)	Washable (W) Disposable (D)	Remote Control	Variable Speed *Remote Only
Delta AP-200	(800) 438-2486	582/402	498	0.2	D	none	N
Delta 50-875	(800) 438-2486	594/437	523	0.3	W	infrared	Y
General Int'l 10-600 M1	(514) 326-1161	402/242	331	3.8	D	radio	Y
General Int'l 10-550 M1	(514) 326-1161	641/383	523	1.2	D	infrared	N
JDS 750-ER	(800) 480-7269	664/514	589	0.3	W	infrared	Y
Jet AFS-1000B	(800) 274-6848	674/383	528	0.8	D	infrared	Y *
Jet AFS-1500	(800) 274-6848	899/737	823	0.65	D	infrared	Y *
Penn State AC620	(800) 377-7297	242/45	139	2.05	W	radio	Y *
Shop Fox W1690	(800) 840-8420	685/484	596	1.8	D	infrared	Y *
Woodtek 923-838	(800) 645-9292	171/99	146	3.6	W	none	N
Woodtek 923-859	(800) 645-9292	271/223	241	6.8	W	radio	N

JDS 750-ER

This is a great all-around air cleaner. The JDS has the two basic requirements sewn up: excellent cfm and great filter performance. Plus, the 750-ER adds an infrared remote, timer, and variable speed.

We wish it had a radio remote, but that's our only complaint.

Delta AP-200

The Delta AP-200 has all the basic requirements at a low price: excellent filtering performance and high cfm. There's no remote control if you're thinking of hanging your machine up out of reach, but the switch is located on the power cord for easy access.

Timer (R)=Remote Only	Ceiling Mounting Hardware Included	Size H x W x L	Decibels (dB)	Comments and Features
N	Y	12" x 24" x 28"	65	Built-in switch in power cord. Electrostatic or charcoal pre-filter available.
Y	Y	12" x 24" x 28"	68	3-speed motor. Timer settings at ½ to 7½ hour settings in ½ hour increments. Built-in dirty-filter indicator. Gaps in filter-flange gasket. Switch on power cord.
Y/R	Y	14" x 24" x 30"	64	Timer settings at 2, 4, 6 and 8 hours. 3-speed fan.
Y	Y	12" x 24" x 28"	65	Single speed. Timer settings at 2, 4 and 8 hours. Gaps in filter-flange gasket.
Y	Y	12" x 24" x 34"	65	3 speeds. Timer settings at 1, 2, 3 and 4 hours. Electrostatic or charcoal pre-filter available.
Y/R	Y	12" x 24" x 30"	66	Timer settings at 2, 4 or 8 hours. 3-speed fan. Electrostatic or charcoal pre-filter available. Gasket around pocket filter frame.
Y/R	Y	16" x 20" x 32"	68	2" thick pre-filter. Timer settings at 2, 4 or 8 hours. 3-speed fan. Comes with two filters, but has the capacity for three. Electrostatic or charcoal pre-filter available.
Y/R	Y	12" x 24" x 30"	57	5 speeds. Gaps in filter-flange gasket. Higher efficiency pocket-filter upgrade available. Timer settings at 2, 4, 6 and 8 hours.
Y/R	Y	12" x 24" x 30"	66	3-speed fan. Gasket around pocket filter frame. Timer settings at 1, 2 and 4 hours.
N	N	12" x 12" x 30"	57	Polyester pocket filter is washable. Switch on power cord.
N	N	12" x 24" x 30"	57	Polyester pocket filter is washable. No pull chain or cord switch for manual operation. 1-micron upgrade filter available.

by ED KRAUSE

Air Scrubber Trio

THREE SHOP-MADE MACHINES THAT CLEAR THE AIR.

Dust haze. Even if you have a dust collection system you've probably found yourself in the middle of it. This fine dust settles onto all the surfaces of your shop where it is a fire hazard (as well as a nuisance) and can lead to respiratory problems. A strategically placed air scrubber can trap much of this dust, keeping your shop cleaner and safer.

Here are three shop-built air scrubber designs: a between-the-joists design for small shops with limited headroom; a hanging model for larger shops; and a benchtop model to catch dust near its source. Each scrubber is based on a kit available from Penn State Industries (see Sources, page 132).

Once you've gathered your materials, you can build any one of these scrubbers in a day. The benchtop and between-the-joists models can be built for $150, the larger model for $220. If you are resourceful enough to find a used furnace blower and use shop scrap, any model can be built for $60.

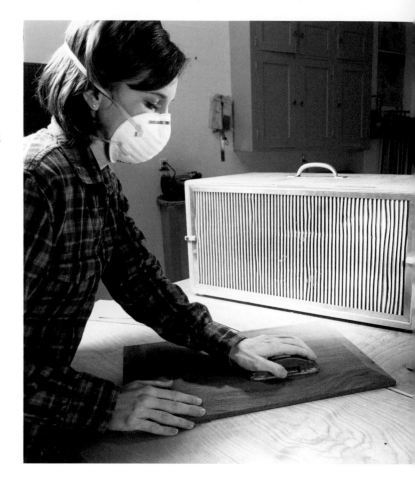

Although these designs are similar to scrubbers available commercially, our scrubbers either cost less or have better features. To make it easy for you to find components, we've used kits and filters available through catalogs. Remember that no air scrubber is a substitute for a dust collector attached to your machines. It is always best to catch dust at its source, before it becomes airborne (see Q&A, page 85). However, an air scrubber can trap much of the fine dust that eludes your primary dust-collection system.

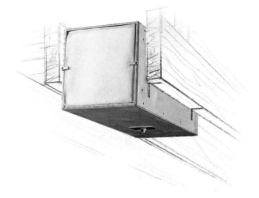

WHICH DESIGN IS BEST FOR YOUR SHOP?

These scrubbers are variations of the same machine, differing in size and where they are placed in your shop. Choose the one that'll work best for you.

The benchtop model is small enough to be used where it's needed, whether it be on your bench when hand sanding, or placed on a stool near your lathe. The between-the-joists model is ideal for a small (500 sq. ft.) basement shop with low ceilings. The larger model has two blower fans enabling it to clean air in a shop twice as large (up to 1,000 sq. ft.) as the other two models.

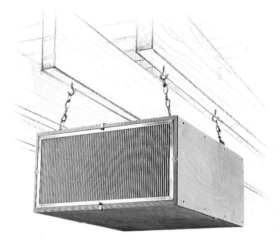

The capacity of your scrubber is another important consideration. For occasional woodworking you need a scrubber that can recirculate all the air in your shop six times every hour or once every 10 minutes. A scrubber's performance is measured by the number of cubic feet per minute (cfm) of air it can handle.

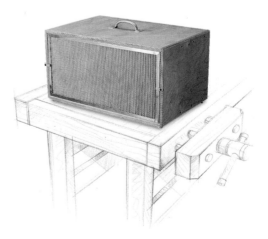

EDITOR: DAVE MUNKITTRICK • ART DIRECTION: JOEL SPIES • PHOTOGRAPHY: BILL ZUEHLKE • ILLUSTRATION: JAN BOER & FRANK ROHRBACH

You can determine exactly how many cfm are required to change the air in your shop six times every hour by measuring the cubic feet of air space in your shop (LxWxH) and dividing that number by 10 (professional woodworkers should divide by 6). For example, if your shop floor space is 25 ft. by 20 feet and your ceilings are 8-ft. high, then your cfm requirements are: 20" x 25" x 8" = 4,000 cubic ft./10 minutes which is 400 cfm. Each of the motors in the Penn State kits are rated at 465 cfm, which is adequate to handle a 500-sq.-ft. shop with 8- to 9-ft. ceilings. For a 1,000-sq.- ft. shop, use two of the single-blower units or build the larger double-blower unit. When in doubt, over do it. This is one case where more is definitely better.

ABOUT FILTERS

There are usually two filters used in an air scrubber: a pre-filter and a pocket filter. The pre-filter prolongs the life of the pocket filter by capturing most of the larger particles first. The pocket filter has a much greater surface area for trapping the finer dust.

To make a scrubber small enough to fit on a bench we substituted a 4-in. pleated filter for the pocket filter. Pleated filters can provide as much or more filter area as pocket filters and are available from Grainger in different levels of efficiency. For our air scrubber we chose a 75-percent efficient filter ($28) which is more efficient than the pocket filters found in most air scrubbers on the market. A 90- to 95-percent efficient filter is available for $84. If you're willing to fork over the money, it'll last longer and catch finer dust.

THE FINISHING TOUCHES

Mount the between-the-joists scrubber with corner brackets (page 106). The larger model should be hung using eye bolts, ceiling hooks, and chain. Add handles and rubber feet to the benchtop model so it can be used vertically or horizontally. It's best to place a scrubber where you make the most dust, and as low as is feasible. None of the three models are heavy, but mounting the overhead models safely is a two-person job.

ADD-ON FEATURES

Add ribbons to the exhaust louvers so you know when it's time to replace or clean your filters (photo page 97). A timer switch enables you to leave the scrubber on when you're not in the shop. The exhaust port of the air scrubber can be ducted outside, like a bathroom fan, to vent low-concentration fumes when brushing or rag-applying finish. The cost for parts is less than $30. To make, simply cut a piece of plywood slightly smaller than the back of the scrubber to use as a mounting flange for the stack boot. Cut an opening in the flange to allow the boot to fit through. Attach the boot to the inside of the cutout with silicone caulk and screws. To hook up the stack boot for outside venting, simply screw on the flange over the exhaust port with a pair of screws. Be sure to remove your pocket filter to help increase airflow when operating your scrubber as a vent. When you're done venting, simply unscrew the mounting flange, replace your pocket filter and you're back to scrubbing the air in your shop. Now you can breathe easier.

MAKING THE SCRUBBERS

All three models are similarly built.

1. Cut plywood to size. We used Baltic birch, (see Sources, page 132) but any ½-in. plywood will work.

2. Cut the cleats to length.

3. Glue and nail cleats to the top and bottom. Be sure to position the cleats precisely, as shown for each model, to allow room for the filters, stops and gaskets on the intake end and for the back and gasket on the exhaust end.

4. Glue and nail the long stops at the end of each pair of cleats.

5. Use screws to attach the sides to the cleats on the top and bottom.

6. Glue and nail the short vertical stops on the exhaust and intake ends.

7. Lay out the motor flange location on the inside of the back. Set the motor in place and mark the screw hole locations. Make lines ¾-in. inside the motor flange outline for the exhaust port cutout. Cut holes for the exhaust port and electrical box with a jigsaw.

8. Drill bolt holes for the motor. The holes need to be countersunk on the outside face of the back to allow for the exhaust louvers.

9. Mount the motor to the back.

10. Mount the electrical box and wire according to your choice of switches. (Between-the-joists model must be wired after the back is attached.)

11. Apply gasket to back stops.

12. Fasten the back to the scrubber with screws.

13. Screw the exhaust louvers over the port.

14. Add the filter clips and apply gasket material to the filter stops. Install the filters.

15. Ease the edges with a router and a ⅛-in. round-over bit or sandpaper.

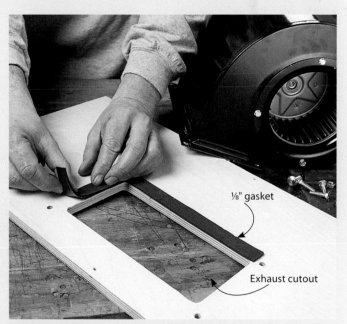

⅛" gasket

Exhaust cutout

Apply gasket material around the cutout after the bolt holes have been drilled. Be sure to countersink the holes on the outside face of the back or the bolt heads will interfere with mounting the exhaust grate.

Between-the-Joists Exploded View

The between-the-joists model is especially well suited for small shops with low ceilings. Mount to joists with corner brackets.

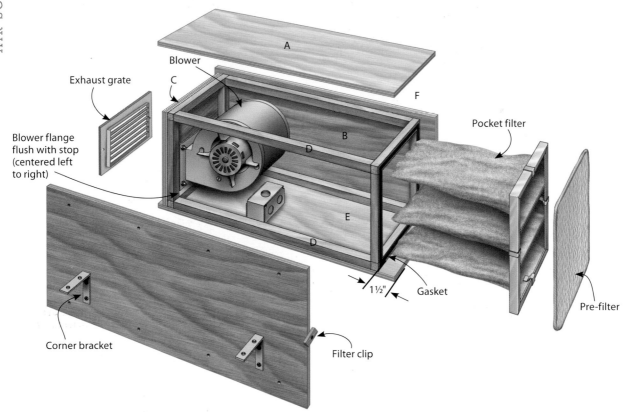

Blower

Exhaust grate

Blower flange flush with stop (centered left to right)

Pocket filter

Pre-filter

1½"

Gasket

Corner bracket

Filter clip

CUTTING LIST

Overall Dimensions: 12¾"H x 12¾"W x 30"D

Part	Name	Quantity	Dimensions	Material
A	Top & Bottom	2	½" x 11¾" x 30"	Baltic birch ply
B	Sides	2	½" x 12¾" x 30"	Baltic birch ply
C	Back	1	½" x 11¾" x 11¾"	Baltic birch ply
D	Cleats	4	¾" x ¾" x 26"	softwood
E	Stops	4	¾" x ¾" x 10¼"	softwood
F	Stops	4	¾" x ¾" x 11¾"	softwood

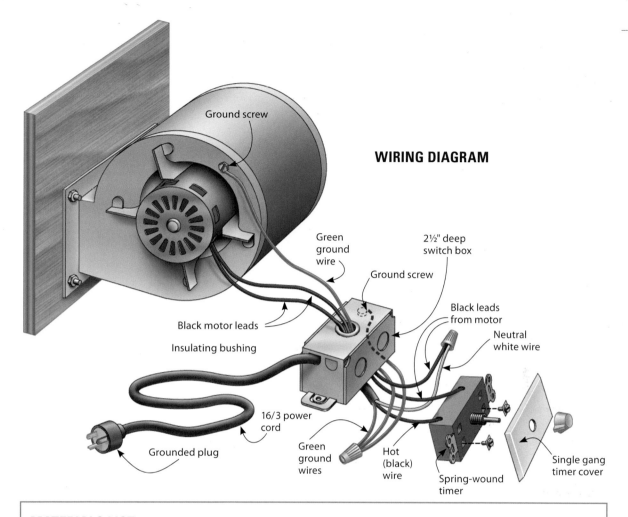

WIRING DIAGRAM

Ground screw

Green ground wire

2½" deep switch box

Ground screw

Black leads from motor

Neutral white wire

Black motor leads

Insulating bushing

16/3 power cord

Grounded plug

Green ground wires

Hot (black) wire

Spring-wound timer

Single gang timer cover

MATERIALS LIST

All Models
- One sheet of ½" plywood
- One 1" x 4" x 8' pine board
- No. 8 x 1" finish head screws
- Four ¼" x ¾" machine bolts, washers and nuts
- Ten ft. ⅛" gasket material
- 16/3 SJ power supply cord
- Wire nuts
- Insulating bushing
- Grounded plug
- Ribbon

Between the Joists
- Penn State Industries kit #ACAW1 (includes motor blower

and exhaust grate)
- 11½" x 11½" pre-filter and pocket filter
- Four 2" corner brackets
- 2½"-deep switch box with integral cable clamps and plaster ears
- Spring-wound timer with hold

Hanging
- Penn State Industries kit #AC930 (includes 2 motor blowers, 2 exhaust grates, pre-filter and pocket filter)
- 3½"-deep switch box with integral cable clamp and plaster ears

- Pull-chain switch
- Single gang blank cover plate (drill for pull chain)
- Four (additional) ¼" x ¾" machine bolts
- Four ¼" x 2" eye bolts
- Twelve ¼" nuts and washers
- Four 60 lb. ceiling hooks
- #2 twin-loop chain
- Four connector links

Benchtop
- Penn State Industries kit #ACAW2 (includes motor blower, exhaust grate and pre-filter)
- 2⅛"-deep handy box with ½" knock-outs

- ½" chase nipple
- ½" close coupling
- ⅜" 2-screw cable clamp
- In-line rocker switch
- Blank handy box cover
- Two 6½" handles
- Eight rubber feet
- 12" x 24" x 4" pleated filter

Add-ons
- 10" x 3¼" x 4" stack boot
- Flexible dryer vent hose
- Hose clamp
- Remote control

Hanging Exploded View

The larger shop model has double blowers for more air volume.

Mount below joists using ceiling hooks, eye-bolts and chain.

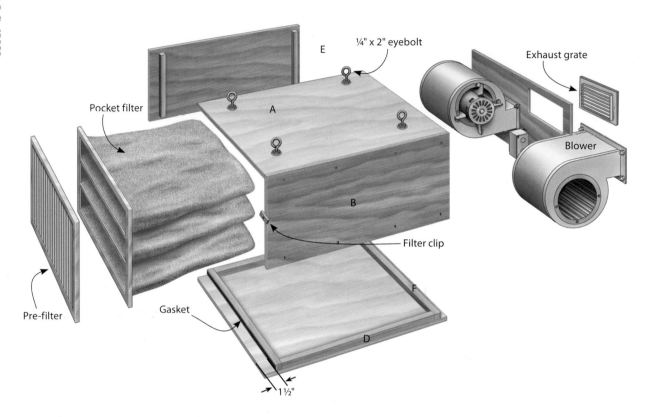

Pocket filter

¼" x 2" eyebolt

E

A

Exhaust grate

B

Blower

Pre-filter

Filter clip

Gasket

F

D

1½"

CUTTING LIST

Overall Dimensions: 12¾"H x 24¾"W x 30"D

Part	Name	Quantity	Dimensions	Material
A	Top & Bottom	2	½" x 23¾" x 30"	Baltic birch ply
B	Sides	2	½" x 12¾" x 30"	Baltic birch ply
C	Back	1	½" x 11¾" x 23¾"	Baltic birch ply
D	Cleats	4	¾" x ¾" x 26"	softwood
E	Stops	4	¾" x ¾" x 10¼"	softwood
F	Stops	4	¾" x ¾" x 23¾"	softwood

DETAIL 1
BACK CUTOUT

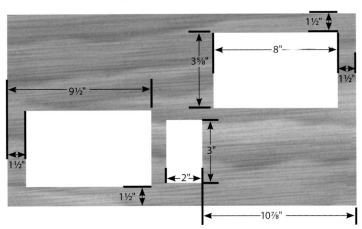

1½"

8"

3⅝"

1½"

9½"

1½"

3"

2"

1½"

10⅞"

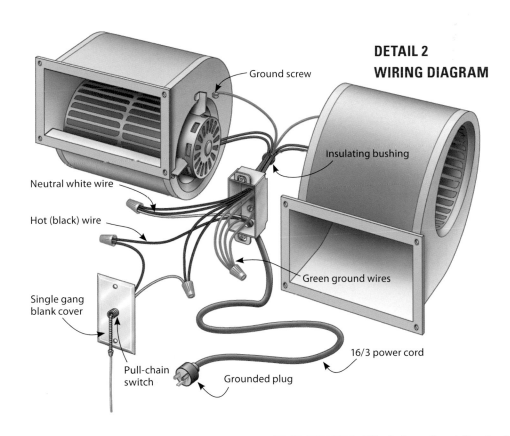

DETAIL 2
WIRING DIAGRAM

Ground screw

Insulating bushing

Neutral white wire

Hot (black) wire

Green ground wires

Single gang
blank cover

16/3 power cord

Pull-chain
switch

Grounded plug

Benchtop Exploded View

Benchtop model pulls in dust where you make it.

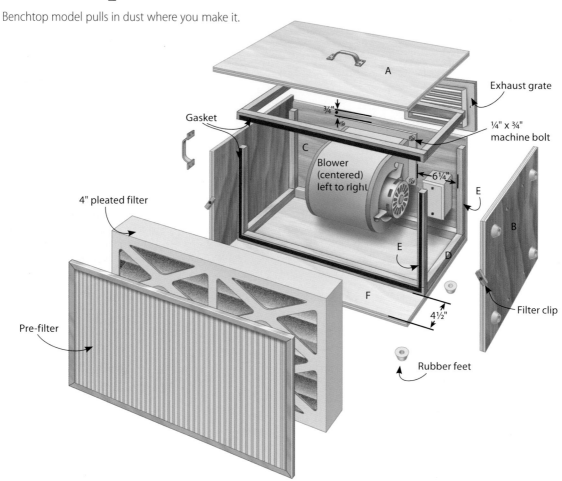

Exhaust grate

Gasket

¾"

¼" x ¾"
machine bolt

4" pleated filter

C

Blower
(centered)
left to right

6¼"

E

E

B

D

F

4½"

Filter clip

Pre-filter

Rubber feet

A

CUTTING LIST

Overall Dimensions: 12¾"H x 24¾"W x 15½"D

Part	Name	Quantity	Dimensions	Material
A	Top & Bottom	2	½" x 23¾" x 15½"	Baltic birch ply
B	Sides	2	½" x 12¾" x 15½"	Baltic birch ply
C	Back	1	½" x 11¾" x 23¾"	Baltic birch ply
D	Cleats	4	¾" x ¾" x 8½"	softwood
E	Stops	4	¾" x ¾" x 10¼"	softwood
F	Stops	4	¾" x ¾" x 23¾"	softwood

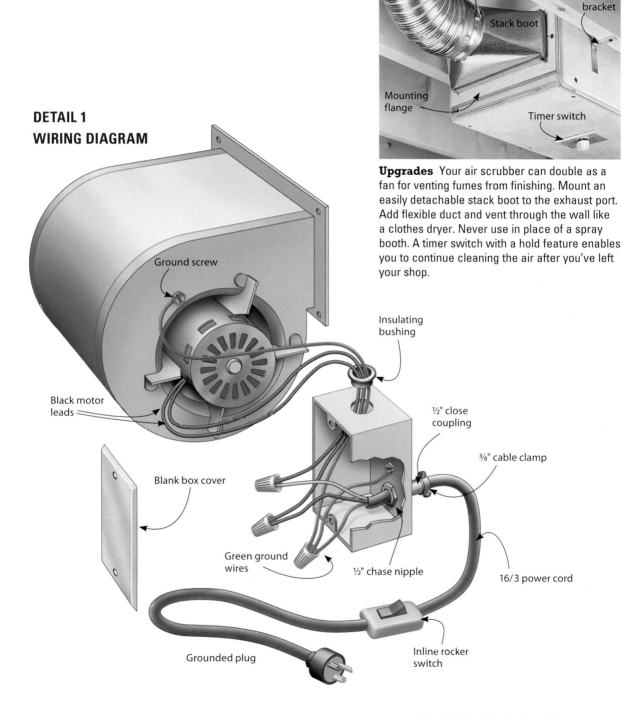

Flexible dryer
vent hose

Corner
bracket

Stack boot

Mounting
flange

Timer switch

Upgrades Your air scrubber can double as a
fan for venting fumes from finishing. Mount an
easily detachable stack boot to the exhaust port.
Add flexible duct and vent through the wall like
a clothes dryer. Never use in place of a spray
booth. A timer switch with a hold feature enables
you to continue cleaning the air after you've left
your shop.

DETAIL 1
WIRING DIAGRAM

Ground screw

Insulating
bushing

Black motor
leads

½" close
coupling

⅜" cable clamp

Blank box cover

Green ground
wires

½" chase nipple

16/3 power cord

Grounded plug

Inline rocker
switch

by RALPH SCHAFER

No-Hassle Filter Cleaning

MODIFIED VACUUM WAND DOESN'T GET STUCK

My air filter works great and sure makes my shop a cleaner and healthier place to work. But cleaning the pleated filter was always a problem. Blowing or shaking it out just made a big mess. I tried vacuuming it, but my vacuum wand would attach itself to the filter like a leech.

I tamed the beast by drilling some ¾-in. holes in the sides of the wand. Now, I just shake the wand around inside the filter and it clears out the dust without clinging to the filter. The number of holes you put in the wand depends on how powerful your vacuum is. Drill just enough holes so the wand doesn't stick to the filter.

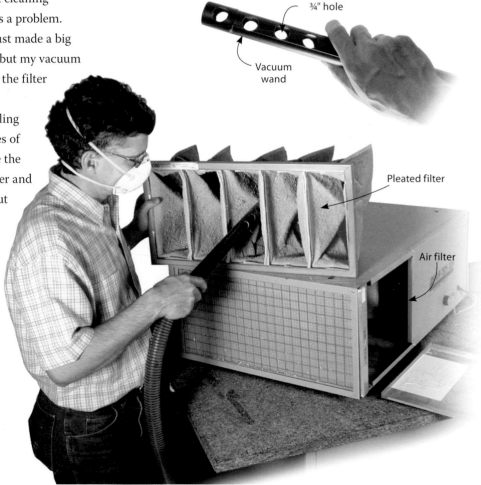

¾" hole

Vacuum wand

Pleated filter

Air filter

by RALPH SCHAFER

Electrostatic Prefilter Advantages

YOU CAN WASH IT AND REUSE IT

Q I don't see anything special about the electrostatic prefilter that came with my air cleaner. There's no wire or contact point that would tell me it's electro-anything. Is this really any different than an ordinary filter?

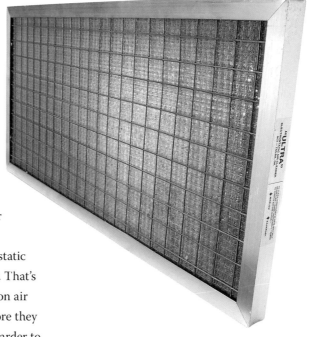

A Although your prefilter is referred to as an electrostatic filter, the only electricity involved is static. When your fan is operating, the air passing over the filter media generates a static charge that attracts and holds dust particles. It's the same type of charge that causes a balloon to stick to the wall after you've rubbed it across your hair a few times.

For a woodworker, the main advantage of an electrostatic prefilter is that it can be washed and reused repeatedly. That's why electrostatic filters are typically used as prefilters on air scrubbers. Prefilters catch the larger dust particles before they plug up the finer pocket filters inside (which are a lot harder to clean). It's important to wash your electrostatic filter often for two reasons: 1. It keeps airflow at a maximum. 2. An electrostatic filter's effectiveness decreases as the filter loads with dust. That's because the media has become insulated by the dust, thus reducing the static charge.

EDITOR: DAVE MUNKITTRICK • ART DIRECTION: JOHN CROMIE • PHOTOGRAPHY: RAMON MOEENO

Compressed Air

Dust control equipment works mainly by drawing debris-laden air through the equipment, returning cleaned air to the workshop. But since we're talking about air movement, it's just as valuable to be able to move it in the other direction. That's why many woodworkers add air compressors to the workshop. A compressor may be the only way to blow dust and debris out of a fitting or a furniture assembly. More than that, though, air compressors allow you to spray finishes and drive air-powered tools, which in most cases are lighter and more efficient than their electrical counterparts.

《These three air compressors pack enough punch to spray finishes and drive air-powered shaping tools.

by RICHARD TENDICK

Tool Review: Small Air Compressors

5 EASY QUESTIONS TO CHOOSE THE RIGHT ONE

Equipping your shop with a small, portable air compressor opens the door to a whole line of time-saving pneumatic tools. You can use a brad nailer or stapler to quickly assemble jigs, furniture, and shop projects. For more exotic uses, you can run a vacuum-bag veneering system or air-powered clamps.

And you can use your compressor around the house for putting up trim, building a deck, inflating car tires and basketballs, and so on.

Buying a small compressor can make your head spin. Dozens of models are available, all varying slightly, ranging from $115 to $350. But your search doesn't have to be difficult. If you know what you plan to use an air compressor for, I'll help you figure out what type to get.

Like a good sales clerk, I'll ask you a series of basic questions to narrow your choices. You don't need to know much about compressors to answer. When you're done, you should know exactly what kind of compressor to buy. When you go shopping, you'll find a few models that fit the bill—just pick the best value.

1 WHAT TOOLS WILL YOU USE?

Figure out the amount of air you'll need

When you shop for a compressor, the most important number to look for is the amount of cubic feet per minute (cfm) it delivers at 90 pounds per square inch (psi). Usually, the most prominent number you see on a box is the machine's horsepower. Everybody is familiar with horsepower ratings for other tools, but for compressors, it's not the most helpful guide. Stick to the cfm rating.

The cfm rating indicates the volume of air a compressor can supply in one minute. Air-powered tools have different cfm requirements. If you're going to run a brad nailer from your compressor, for example, you may only need a 1- to 2-cfm unit. A framing nailer requires a 2- to 4-cfm compressor.

Spray guns require 7 to 11 cfm, random-orbit sanders, up to 15 cfm. If you plan on using these tools, you'll need a much larger compressor than the small ones covered here, but the five questions still apply.

1 to 2 cfm

A 1- to 2-cfm compressor can drive one brad nailer or one finish nailer.

Multiple tools require more air

Running more than one tool from a compressor increases the amount of air you'll need. If you work in a small production shop, work on a job site, or plan a home-remodeling job on which two, three, or four people will be using air nailers, a small compressor may still provide adequate air, but each additional tool puts a heavier burden on the compressor. Shooting dozens of brads or staples in a short amount of time has the same effect.

It's better to buy a compressor with a higher cfm rating than one that marginally meets your requirements. Underestimating your air delivery needs will reduce your tool's performance, possibly shorten your compressor's life and, if the compressor runs frequently, create a very noisy shop.

Air flow affects performance

When their tanks are fully charged, all small compressors deliver enough pressure to run most woodworking air-powered tools. But your tools won't perform well if you have a compressor whose cfm rating is too low.

Let's imagine you're driving brads. As you draw air from the tank, its pressure drops until the compressor's motor starts to run. If the compressor isn't able to supply enough air to the tank while you continue to work, the tank's pressure will drop further, even though the motor is running. The nailer may not get enough air pressure to drive a brad all the way in. You have to stop work so the compressor can rebuild pressure. Insufficient air flow prevents your tools from working at their full capacity and slows you down.

2 to 4 cfm

A 2- to 4-cfm compressor can drive two brad nailers, two finish nailers, or one framing nailer.

A 4- to 5-cfm compressor can drive four brad nailers, four finish nailers, or two framing nailers.

2 HOW HARD WILL YOU USE IT?

Choose the tank's size

Tank shapes and sizes vary quite a bit. When you're shopping, don't get hung up on choosing among pancake, single, or double tanks. Pay more attention to the tank's volume and less to its shape.

A tank's shape doesn't affect a compressor's ability to deliver air. Double tanks, for example, don't offer some secret advantage. A pancake or single-tank compressor performs just as well as a double-tank compressor.

The larger the tank's volume, no matter what its shape, the less often the compressor will kick in. If you're going to be a hard user, continuously shooting brads, staples, or nails, go for the largest tank in your cfm range. If you'll be a light user, shooting a dozen or so brads at a time, you'll be OK with a smaller volume tank. It will be more compact and weigh less.

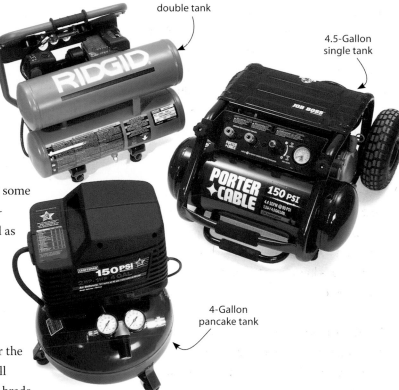

4-Gallon double tank

4.5-Gallon single tank

4-Gallon pancake tank

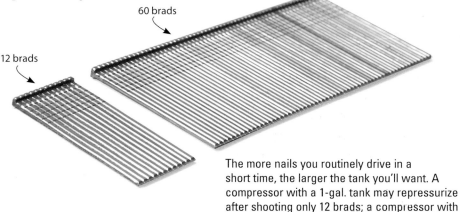

60 brads

12 brads

The more nails you routinely drive in a short time, the larger the tank you'll want. A compressor with a 1-gal. tank may repressurize after shooting only 12 brads; a compressor with a 6-gal. tank may handle as many as 60 brads before the tank must be repressurized.

3 WHICH IS MORE IMPORTANT TO YOU—LONG LIFE OR LOW MAINTENANCE?

Decide between an oil-lubricated or oilless unit

Most oil-lubricated compressors can be run longer per hour than oilless compressors can. They have a very long life but require routine maintenance. On occasion, they might spit oil on your project.

Oilless compressors shouldn't be run more than 30 minutes per hour, on average. They have a shorter life, but don't require much maintenance and won't spit oil. Oilless compressors generally cost about $50 less than oil-lubricated units with similar cfm ranges and tank sizes.

Duty cycle

This term refers to the length of time in one hour that a compressor should be allowed to run without stopping. Most oil-lubricated compressors can run 45 minutes out of every hour, giving them a 75-percent duty cycle. Most jobs in a one-person woodshop don't require a compressor to run this much, but when a compressor's air flow is barely adequate for a spraying or sanding job, or its tank volume is small, an oil-lubricated unit is the best choice. Most oilless compressors have a 50-percent duty cycle. They should be allowed to stop a total of 30 minutes out of each hour of use to cool down.

compressor dipstick

Life span

A well-maintained oil-lubricated compressor has approximately a 4,000-hour running-time life expectancy; an oilless unit will run from 500 to 2,000 hours. Let's put those numbers in perspective: To reach 500 hours, the bare minimum, you would have to run your compressor a total of 2 hours a week for 5 years. Many oilless compressors are inexpensive and easy to rebuild (see photo, right). Rebuild kits aren't available for all models, however. Oil-lubricated compressors are not easy to rebuild. You can do it yourself, but you'll need special tools. Professional compressor-repair shops in your area may be able to rebuild your unit.

Maintenance

An oil-lubricated compressor should have its oil changed regularly (see photo, below right). You should check its oil level, too, from time to time. Oilless compressors don't need to be monitored this closely.

Oil spits

An oil-lubricated compressor may spray tiny droplets of oil. This should happen only on rare occasions, but an older compressor with a worn cylinder is more likely than a new one to suffer this problem. You can often sand or wash oil droplets off your project.

Piston   Cylinder

Oil-less compressors are easy to rebuild. Usually, all you need is a new cylinder and a new piston to extend the compressor's life. The set costs less than $50. Replacing these parts doesn't require special tools or skills.

Oil-lubricated compressors require regular maintenance. Depending on the compressor, you should change its oil every three months to a year or after 100 to 300 hours of use.

4 WILL YOU BE MOVING IT OUTSIDE YOUR SHOP?

Determine whether weight matters

If you plan to park your compressor in one spot and rarely move it, its weight isn't important. But if you foresee using your compressor upstairs and downstairs, indoors and outdoors, its weight can make a big difference.

Small compressors range from 20 to 90 lbs. Obviously, it's much easier to carry a 20-lb. unit up a flight of stairs than a 90-lb. unit. Some heavier compressors come with wheels and a long handle to make them more portable, but these make the machine larger and more difficult to store.

Store a lightweight compressor just about anywhere. Park it on a shelf to save space. If it's secure, it can run up there, too.

20 lbs.

72 lbs.

5 HOW DUSTY IS YOUR SHOP?

Inspect the intake filter

Dust can shorten your compressor's life. A good intake filter that's routinely cleaned offers the best protection.

Dust and dirt drawn into a compressor act like sand caught between the pump's piston and cylinder. They grind away with each stroke, reducing the motor's efficiency. The intake filter's job is to remove dust from the air before it reaches the pump.

Intake filters vary widely among compressors. Unfortunately, you can't easily upgrade the filter after you buy a compressor. Since you do know how dusty it gets in your shop, you can choose a specific air compressor by which type of filter it has. The larger a filter's surface area, the longer it will remain effective between cleanings. A pleated-paper cartridge filter is best, having the largest surface area. Many compressors have foam filters, which are less efficient at trapping very small dust particles. Some compressors don't have any filter at all.

Filters require regular cleaning. A clogged filter blocks the free flow of air to the compressor, requiring it to work harder, which could damage your compressor.

Portable Compressor Station

I have to pack all my tools into the back of my garage when I'm not woodworking. To conserve space, I bought a pancake-style compressor for its compact size and portability. At 55 lbs. it's portable, but lugging it around is no picnic.

To make it easier to move, I put it in a small open cabinet on wheels. I bolted the compressor to the bottom to keep it from vibrating its way out. To make the setup even more versatile, I mounted an air hose reel on top. I put a 12-in. lazy-Susan bearing between the hose reel and cabinet so I can unroll the hose in any direction.

—*Forrest Nerbitt*

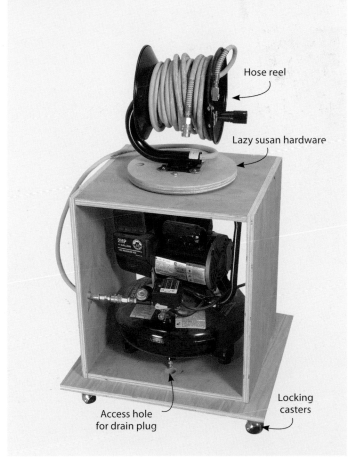

Hose reel

Lazy susan hardware

Access hole for drain plug

Locking casters

MORE SPECS TO CONSIDER

Small, low-rpm machines run more quietly

A loud compressor in a small shop can drive a person nuts. Fortunately, some compressors are much quieter than others. Their sound-pressure levels vary from about 80 to 90 dBA, a significant difference that's roughly equivalent to the noise of an idling tablesaw compared with the same saw ripping thick hardwood. As you might expect, 1- to 2-cfm compressors are generally the least noisy. Unfortunately, noise levels measured in decibels aren't widely reported in manufacturer's spec sheets. Try before you buy.

The speed at which a compressor runs also affects its noise level. Some compressors run at 1,720 rpm, while others run at 3,450 rpm. Low-speed machines are noticeably quieter.

Knee-Saving Compressor Drain

Crouching to operate my compressor's drain valve was no big deal until my football-ravaged knees started acting up. To keep from grimacing in the sawdust, I devised a more civilized way to clear the tank. I replaced the drain valve with a 90-degree elbow, a 200-psi-rated reinforced hose and a ball valve. Barb fittings on the elbow and ball valve and clamps on the hose keep everything air tight. I chose a ball valve instead of an air nozzle so no one would mistake my new drain hose for a regular air hose.

—*Richard Fenwick*

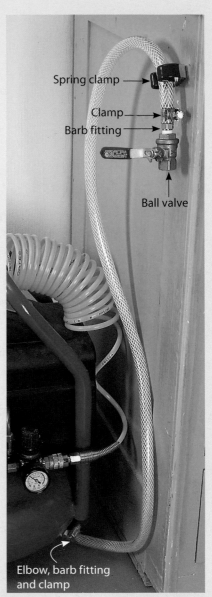

Spring clamp

Clamp

Barb fitting

Ball valve

Elbow, barb fitting and clamp

Higher pressure increases air in the tank

Some compressors are built to handle much higher maximum pressure than others. Overall, maximum air pressure ranges from 100 to 150 psi. You don't need this increased pressure to run most woodworking tools, but it does have a definite benefit: a 150-psi tank will cycle on and off less often, because it contains more air than a 100-psi tank of the same volume. A 1-gal. tank pressurized at 150 psi contains about 11 gal. of air, while the same tank at 100 psi contains only 7 gal. A high-pressure oilless compressor will have more time to cool down between cycles, which extends its life.

More horsepower requires more amperage

The more air a compressor delivers, the more horsepower and amperage it needs. A ½-hp compressor typically draws about 4 amps, a 1-hp compressor, 10 amps, and a 1.6-hp compressor, 15 amps.

A compressor that draws 15 amps should be run on a dedicated 20-amp circuit to avoid blowing a fuse or tripping a breaker. Manufacturers recommend that you do not use an extension cord on a high-amp unit. (You can, however, use a long hose to deliver air far away from a compressor; see "Plumb Your Shop with Air," page 126.) Check out the amperage of your shop and home circuits before buying a high-amp machine.

by RICHARD TENDICK

Plumb Your Shop with Air

FLEXIBLE HOSE SAVES TIME AND MONEY

Moments after I tripped over the air hose and dropped an armload of boards, I decided it was time to plumb my shop for air. I was tired of having 50 ft. of hose on the floor and dashing back to the compressor to adjust the line pressure. I knew a permanent system could deliver the right amount of air where and when I needed it—without a big hose snaked dangerously across the floor.

Every article I read on plumbing air lines advised using either iron or copper. Because my basement shop holds a lot of obstructions, using iron or copper would result in a whole lot of threading or soldering of short little pieces. Besides, copper and iron fittings are costly.

Ultimately, I decided on a solution I had used many times in my 27 years as a manufacturing plant engineer. When installing printing presses and other large machines, I used rubber air hose as a flexible pipe to route compressed air in and through the equipment without having to do a lot of complicated plumbing.

That approach would certainly work with all the obstructions in my shop. I chose a rubber hose rated for 250 pounds per square inch (psi), plenty for my little pancake compressor. The ½-in. inside diameter meant no reduction in air pressure would occur along the length of the run.

Tip:

Check for air leaks by spraying a mixture of detergent and water at every connection; bubbles will indicate escaping air.

HARDWARE LIST

Part	Name	Source/Model #	Price
A	½" compressed-air filter	MSC #01780337	$44
B	¼" regulator with gauge	MSC #04290490	$31
C	¼" ball valve	MSC #37009727	$9
D	½" ball valve	MSC #37009743	$9
E	½" air hose (red)	MSC #48563720	$1 per ft.
F	½" x ½" barbed fitting	MSC #48755516	$1.50
G	#8 hose clamp	MSC #48706097	$0.50
H	¼" x 12' coiled hose and gun	MSC #48670400	$21
J	¼" coupler	MSC #AP79863049	$14
K	¼" connector	MSC #AP79863148	$3
L	½" x ¼" reducer bushing	MSC #79870341	$1.50
M	¼" close pipe nipple	MSC #48772180	$0.60
N	¼" x 2" nipple	MSC #02204717	$1.50
P	¼" 90° elbow	MSC #02201234	$3.50
Q	½" x ½" female adapter	Home center	$1.50
R	½" copper tee	Home center	$1
S	½" copper pipe	Home center	$3.50 for 10 ft.
T	½" copper hanger	Home center	$1 for 10
U	½" plastic hanger	Home center	$1.50 for 10
V	¾" plastic hanger	Home center	$1.50 for 10
W	¼" x 12' coiled hose	MSC #88121835	$25

Source: MSC Industrial Supply, (800) 645-7270, www.mscdirect.com

The Parts

Starting at the compressor, the air is filtered for oil and debris before it enters the system. At the two drops, the transition between the rubber hose and the solid pipe is made with a barbed hose fitting (F) and a hose clamp (G). The barbs grip the inside of the hose when the hose clamp is applied, resulting in a tight seal. Copper joints are joined with solder. Threaded brass fittings are sealed with Teflon tape wrapped around the threads.

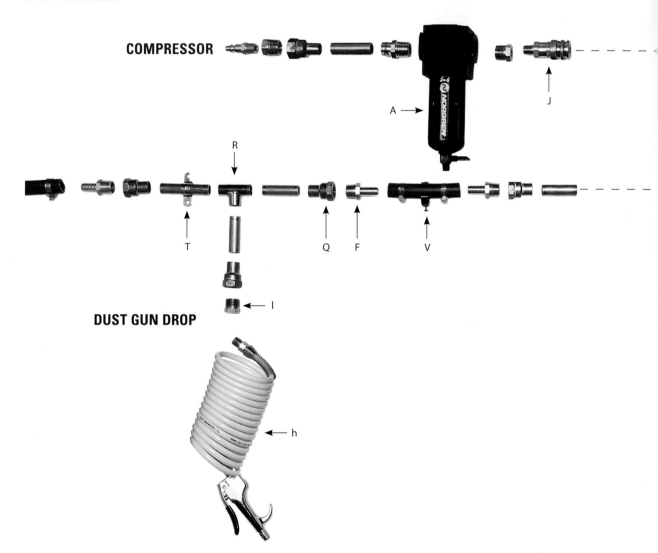

COMPRESSOR

A

J

R

T

Q

F

V

I

DUST GUN DROP

h

There are five different coupling styles in the ¼-in. size. The three most popular styles of fittings: industrial, automotive, and ARO. Most woodworking tools use the industrial style.

Industrial style   Automotive style   ARO style

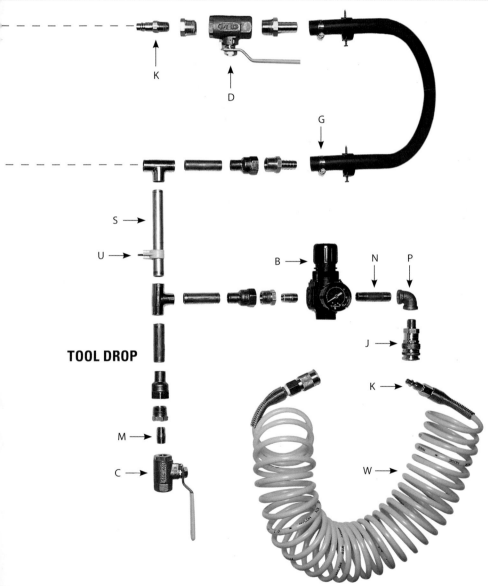

K

D

G

S

U

B

N

P

J

K

TOOL DROP

M

C

W

The Layout

Rubber air hose is an easy, economical, and industry-proven method of routing compressed-air lines in your shop. The rigid copper drops are installed on the wall where needed. The hose can then be routed in a matter of minutes, using a knife to cut the hose and a screwdriver to tighten the hose clamps. The copper drops can be soldered on your bench before they're installed.

An **air filter** keeps water and oil out of the lines.

Copper drops bring the air to work areas and provide rigidity for easy tool hookup.

A **ball valve locks** compressed air in the lines so you can disconnect the compressor from the system and go mobile.

A **shelf** for the compressor frees floor space.

Quick disconnects are set 45 degrees from the wall to prevent skinned knuckles.

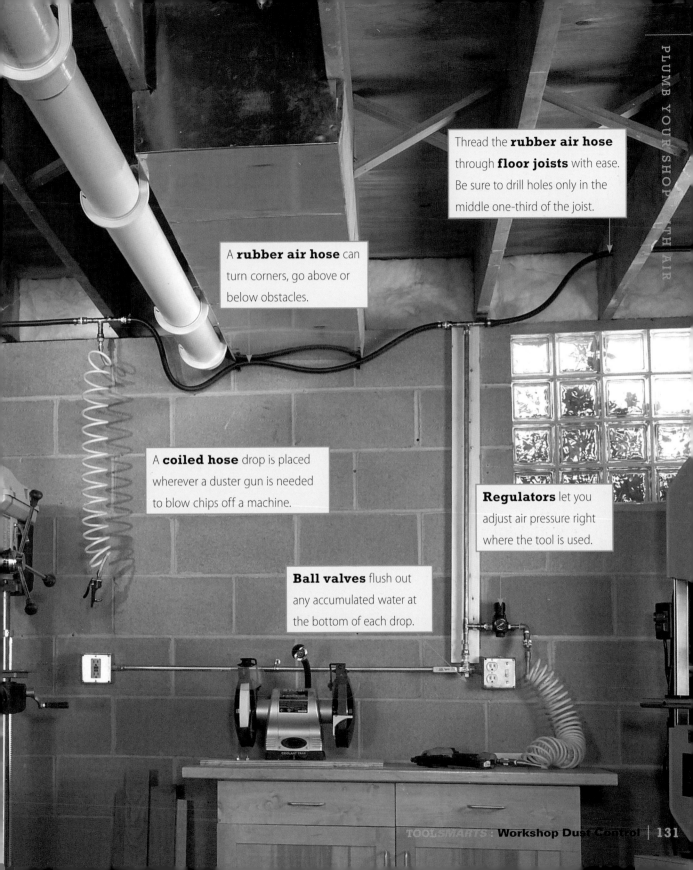

Thread the **rubber air hose** through **floor joists** with ease. Be sure to drill holes only in the middle one-third of the joist.

A **rubber air hose** can turn corners, go above or below obstacles.

A **coiled hose** drop is placed wherever a duster gun is needed to blow chips off a machine.

Regulators let you adjust air pressure right where the tool is used.

Ball valves flush out any accumulated water at the bottom of each drop.

Sources

CENTRAL DUST COLLECTION SYSTEMS

Oneida Air Systems
800-732-4065
www.oneida-air.com

Delta Machinery
800-438-2486
www.deltawoodworking.com

Grizzly
800-523-4777
www.grizzlyindustrial.com

Jet Tools
800-274-6848
www.jettools.com

JDS
800-480-7269
www.jdstools.com

Powermatic
800-248-0144
www.powermatic.com

General International
514-326-1161
www.general.ca

Penn State Industries
800-377-7297
www.pennstateind.com

Laguna Tools
800-234-1976
www.lagunatools.com

SHOP VACUUMS

Ridgid (Home Depot)
888-743-4333
www.ridgid.com

Fein
www.fein.de
800-441-9878

MOTORS, SWITCHES, PARTS

Grainger
www.grainger.com

CARTRIDGE DUST FILTERS

Kufo Industries Corp
888-558-4628
www.kufogroup.com

DUCTS, BLAST GATES, SWITCHES

Lee Valley Tools
800-871-8158

Woodcraft Supply
800-225-1153
www.woodcraft.com

Rockler
800-279-4441
www.rockler.com

Woodworker's Supply (Woodtek)
800-645-9292
www.woodworker.com

RESPIRATORS AND DUST MASKS

Conney Safety Products
800-356-9100
www.conney.com

Triton
888-874-8661
www.tritonwoodworking.com

3M
888-364-3577
www.3m.com

Trend Routing Technology
270-872-4674
www.trend-uk.com

COMPRESSED AIR FITTINGS

MSC Industrial Supply
800-645-7270
www.mscdirect.com

THE *Missing* SHOP MANUAL SERIES

These are the manuals that should have come with your new woodworking tools. In addition to explaining the basics of safety and set-up, each *Missing Shop Manual* covers everything your new tool was designed to do on its own and with the help of jigs & fixtures. No fluff, just straight tool information at your fingertips.

Circular Saws and Jig Saws
From ripping wood to circle cutting, you'll discover the techniques to maximize your saw's performance.

ISBN 978-1-56523-469-7
$9.95 USD • 88 Pages

Drills and Drill Presses
Exert tips and techniques on everything from drilling basic holes and driving screws to joinery and mortising.

ISBN 978-1-56523-472-7
$9.95 USD • 104 Pages

Glue and Clamps
Learn how to get the most out of your clamps and that bottle of glue when you're carving, drilling, and building furniture.

ISBN 978-1-56523-468-0
$9.95 USD • 104 Pages

Table Saw
Whether you're using a bench top, contractor or cabinet saw, get tips on everything from cutting dados and molding to creating jigs.

ISBN 978-1-56523-471-0
$12.95 USD • 144 Pages

Lathe
Maximize your lathe's performance with techniques for everything from sharpening your tools to faceplate, bowl, and spindle turning.

ISBN 978-1-56523-470-3
$12.95 USD • 152 Pages

Back to *Basics*   *Straight Talk for Today's* **Woodworker**

Get *Back to Basics* with the core information you need to succeed. This new series offers a clear road map of fundamental woodworking knowledge on sixteen essential topics. It explains what's important to know now and what can be left for later. Best of all, it's presented in the plain-spoken language you'd hear from a trusted friend or relative. The world's already complicated—your woodworking information shouldn't be.

Constructing Kitchen Cabinets

ISBN 978-1-56523-466-6
$19.95 USD • 144 Pages

Woodworker's Guide to Joinery

ISBN 978-1-56523-462-8
$19.95 USD • 200 Pages

Woodworker's Guide to Wood

ISBN 978-1-56523-464-2
$19.95 USD • 160 Pages

Woodworking Machines

ISBN 978-1-56523-465-9
$19.95 USD • 192 Pages

Setting Up Your Workshop

ISBN 978-1-56523-463-5
$19.95 USD • 152 Pages

Fundamentals of Sharpening

ISBN 978-1-56523-496-3
$19.95 USD • 128 Pages

Woodworker's Guide to Carving

ISBN 978-1-56523-497-0
$19.95 USD • 160 Pages

Look for These Books at Your Local Bookstore or Woodworking Retailer
To order direct, call **800-457-9112** or visit *www.FoxChapelPublishing.com*

By mail, please send check or money order + $4.00 per book for S&H to:
Fox Chapel Publishing, 1970 Broad Street, East Petersburg, PA 17520

Discover these other great books from American Woodworker and Fox Chapel Publishing

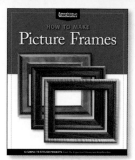

How to Make Picture Frames

12 Simple to Stylish Projects from the Experts at American Woodworker
Edited by Randy Johnson

Add a special touch to cherished photos and artwork with these easy-to-make picture frames.

ISBN: 978-1-56523 – 459-8
$19.95 • 120 Pages

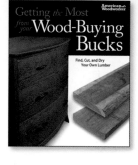

Getting the Most from your Wood-Buying Bucks

Find, Cut, and Dry Your Own Lumber
Edited by Tom Caspar

This handy and essential guide will save you money and expand your wood knowledge.

ISBN: 978-1-56523-460-4
$19.95 • 208 Pages

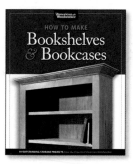

How to Make Bookshelves and Bookcases

19 Outstanding Storage Projects from the Experts at American Woodworker
Edited by Randy Johnson

Build functional yet stylish pieces from a simple wall shelf to a grand bookcase. Features step-by-step instructions, cut-lists, and complete diagrams.

ISBN: 978-1-56523-458-1
$19.95 • 160 Pages

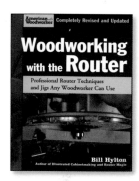

Woodworking with the Router

Professional Router Techniques and Jigs Any Woodworker Can Use
By Bill Hylton

The undisputed champion of router books. Clear, comprehensive and packed with expert tips and techniques.

ISBN: 978-1-56523-438-3
$24.95 • 384 Pages

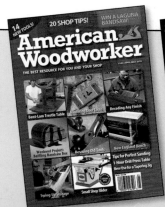

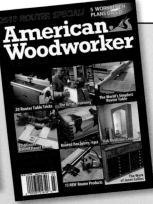

American Woodworker

With American Woodworker, you'll know what the experts know. No other woodworking magazine gives you so many exciting projects, expert tips and techniques, shop-tested tool reviews and smart ways to improve your workshop and make your shop time more satisfying.

Subscribe Today!
Call 1-800-666-3111 or
visit Americanwoodworker.com

Look For These Books at Your Local Bookstore or Woodworking Retailer

To order direct, call **800-457-9112** or visit *www.FoxChapelPublishing.com*

By mail, please send check or money order + $4.00 per book for S&H to:
Fox Chapel Publishing, 1970 Broad Street, East Petersburg, PA 17520